D060755

ANIMALS
ON THE EDGE
REPORTING FROM **EDGE**
THE FRONTLINE OF EXTINCTION

ANIMALS ON THE EDGE

REPORTING FROM THE FRONTLINE OF EXTINCTION

CHRIS WESTON

PHOTOGRAPHS BY CHRIS WESTON AND ART WOLFE

With 179 color photographs

Thames & Hudson

◄◄ *Bornean orangutan mother and baby. The population of Bornean orangutans*
is estimated to be less than 14% of what it was in the mid-20th century.

For Leo – look what we did!
And for Miss Langley – know that
to this child you made a difference.

First published in 2009 in hardcover in the United States of America by
Thames & Hudson Inc., 500 Fifth Avenue, New York, New York 10110

thamesandhudsonusa.com

Library of Congress Catalog Card Number 2008912010

ISBN 978-0-500-54382-5

Printed and bound in Singapore by C S Graphics Pte Ltd

CONTENTS

FOREWORD
DR JANE SMART, IUCN

The diversity of plants and animals that exist in today's world are the product of 3.5 billion years of evolution. These species are the result of evolutionary processes which in more recent times have included the impact of human beings. Current estimates of the number of species range from 5 to 30 million, with a best estimate of 8 to 14 million; of these, only around 1.8 million have been named or 'described'.

While scientists debate how many species exist, there are growing concerns about the rising tide of extinctions. This book focuses attention on some of the terrestrial mammals that are categorized as Endangered or Critically Endangered on The IUCN Red List of Threatened Species™. Although only 2.5% of the world's described species have been assessed so far, The IUCN Red List provides a useful snapshot of what is happening to species today and highlights the urgent need for conservation.

The IUCN Red List is the world's most comprehensive information source on the global conservation status of plant and animal species. It is based on an objective system of assessing the risk of extinction for a species, should no conservation action be taken.

However, The IUCN Red List is more than a register of names and associated threat categories. It is a rich compendium of information on the threats to the featured species, their ecological requirements, where they live, and proposals for conservation actions that can be used to prevent extinctions. It is increasingly used by scientists, governments, NGOs, businesses, and individuals and organizations across civil society for a wide variety of purposes.

The captivating images in this book take us on a journey through many countries, highlighting some of the issues that put these species at risk, meeting people whose daily lives are interlinked with them, and explaining the need for conservation action.

Species *can* recover if we make concerted conservation efforts. In 2008, 37 mammal species improved their conservation status on The IUCN Red List and an estimated 16 bird species have avoided extinction over the last 15 years due to the targeted actions of conservationists. Wildlife conservation works – but to halt the extinction crisis much more needs to be done, and quickly.

Dr Jane Smart OBE
Director, IUCN Biodiversity Conservation Group
Head, IUCN Species Programme

www.iucn.org/species
www.iucnredlist.org

> " WILDLIFE CONSERVATION WORKS – BUT TO HALT THE EXTINCTION CRISIS MUCH MORE NEEDS TO BE DONE, AND QUICKLY. "

◀ *Northern white-cheeked gibbon photographed at dusk. This critically endangered ape, occurring in parts of Southeast Asia, is threatened by habitat loss as well as hunting for food, the pet trade and traditional medicine.*

INTRODUCTION

A few years ago, early in my career as a wildlife photographer, I was on assignment in a then little-known region of Kenya called the Taita Hills reserve. Lying to the west of the Mombasa–Nairobi highway, the reserve is a volcanic landscape, rich in wildlife. More importantly, it dissects East and West Tsavo National Parks, forming part of a wildlife corridor that is an important elephant migration route. I was working on a story about the impact of human encroachment on elephant populations in the region. A few days into my visit we got a call from an official at the Kenya Wildlife Service (KWS) to say that an elephant had been found dead on the edge of a nearby settlement, apparently killed by villagers. As I set off with my guides and camera, I was full of anger at yet another example of human intolerance of wildlife.

At the scene of the incident I took some images amidst the ebb and flow of impassioned, sometimes fiery conversation between the KWS authorities and the villagers. After a time I began mingling with the locals and, with the help of an interpreter, started asking questions, seeking the inside story. That was when I met Matunde, a man who, in one short exchange, was to change entirely my attitude towards the subject of animal/human conflict, and conservation in general; and who, although I didn't know it at the time, was the catalyst for the *Animals on the Edge* project.

Matunde is an uneducated but intelligent man. When we met, he lived in a small hut on an only slightly larger plot of land – about the size of a tennis court – with his wife and five children. On his allotment, to provide for his family and to earn the meagre fees needed to send his two eldest children to the local school – their only hope of a brighter future – Matunde grew lettuces, which he then carted several miles to sell at the nearest market. 'Look at my land,' he said to me. 'I can tell you the value in [Kenyan] shillings of every square foot. If an elephant wanders through here and tramples half my crop, that's not just a few lettuces it's destroyed that I can replace with a quick trip to the local supermarket. That's half my annual income.' He continued: 'Let me ask you, Mr Chris: if someone or something came to your home and took half of your annual income, how would you react? What action would you take – honestly?'

Matunde opened my eyes to the real issues surrounding wildlife conservation. It is no coincidence that the majority of endangered species inhabit areas where people struggle simply to survive. In essence, we will never remove the threats to wildlife unless we fully understand that their root cause, in most cases, is linked to human poverty. That afternoon, during the drive back to camp, I determined that one day I would tell Matunde's story in the context of my work.

I embarked on this book in 2007. Since then, my working life has been a flurry. Few people outside of the photography profession grasp the amount of time and effort – in research, planning and execution – that

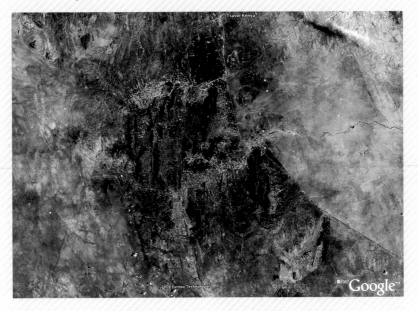

Tsavo, Kenya

2008 Europa Technologies   ©2007 Google™

◀ Taita Hills in Kenya, as revealed by Google Earth satellite photography. It was during an assignment in this part of Kenya that the seed of the idea for this book was sewn.

◀◀ In Madagascar, home of the red ruffed lemur, the average wage is less than US$1 a day: it is no coincidence that most endangered species exist in regions where people face a daily struggle to survive.

With the scope of the project determined, next I spent hours researching species, habitats and locations. This was a long, drawn-out task involving a great deal of time sitting in front of a computer typing variations of search strings into Google, wading through thousands of pages of written material (not all of it well written), and dialling phone numbers to far-flung destinations. I called in favours, conferred with biologist friends and colleagues working in conservation, and spoke to friends of friends of friends and even to the odd government minister. As time went by a plan emerged and a vision for the book took shape. Finally, in December 2007, I booked my first plane tickets, bound for central India to photograph tigers.

goes into the creation of each image. My life has been a blur of airports and aeroplanes interspersed with jungle camps and backstreet hotels. I have visited almost every continent, climbing mountains, crossing plateaus and traversing rivers. I've shinned up trees a hundred feet high, hacked my way through jungles, dug man-size holes, and crawled on all fours across inhospitable terrain. I have ridden elephants, paddled canoes and rafts, and flown in contraptions that should have been grounded long ago. I have been too hot and too cold and many times I've been exhausted and ill. I've been lost, held up at gunpoint, and been stranded in the middle of nowhere with just my cameras and the shirt on my back. I have seen countries transform from kingdom to republic and governments change from left to right. Through all this I had one mission in mind: to visit for myself the frontline in the battle against extinction.

Before embarking on any travels, my initial task was to determine the scope of the project, and to that end I contacted the International Union for Conservation of Nature (IUCN). The IUCN Red List of Threatened Species™ classifies nearly 17,000 animals as threatened to one degree or another; too many to contemplate. I decided to focus on terrestrial mammals categorized as Endangered or Critically Endangered, the two gravest classifications before extinction. Using these new criteria the revised list of subjects extended to over 600 species and subspecies. The final selection in this book runs to over 50 species. Many are iconic, others less well known. Collectively they are only the tip of the iceberg of our contemporary conservation crisis.

I also enlisted the help of my good friend and esteemed colleague Art Wolfe, one of the world's most accomplished nature photographers and a vociferous advocate of the conservation message. I first met Art in London several years ago, when we spent a day exploring the 'nature' of Britain's capital. Since then, our paths have crossed several times and I am both delighted and honoured that he agreed to contribute to and support this project.

Talking of external contributors, the critical input of the many people who have aided the project along the way must also be recognized. Wildlife photography is rarely a solitary pursuit. In India, I was greatly indebted to my fixer, Nanda Rana, who talked our way into opportunities that would certainly otherwise have passed me by. In Nepal, it would have been impossible to photograph the Asiatic buffalo without my 'Buffalo Soldiers' – the team of herders who coaxed the animals towards my hidden cameras, at great risk to themselves and in conditions far from conducive to the physical exertion required. There are many such stories associated with this project – from tracking primates in Africa to big cats in Asia and beyond – and I am grateful to all the people who helped me in the field and who are acknowledged at the end of the book.

This project has proved to be an unceasing journey of discovery. During its course, I have been both encouraged and disheartened by what I have encountered. I have marvelled at the success of efforts to halt the decline in the population of mountain gorillas in Rwanda, a country that as recently as 1994 endured one of the most horrific genocides ever recorded, and yet is now a stable democracy. Similarly, in Gabon, one of the world's poorest countries, President El Hadj Bongo in 2002 set aside 25,000 km² (10,000 miles²) of the country's land to form a national park system protecting some of Africa's last remaining pristine wilderness, forsaking the easy dollar to be gained from logging and agriculture in preference to preserving the beauty of his country's natural resources. This was an immensely courageous decision that should protect an abundance of wildlife for generations to come.

At the same time, I have been profoundly disturbed by the prevalence of corruption, hypocrisy, self-interest and posturing; and by the weakness and Machiavellian machinations of many of the governments and organizations on whom the future of our wildlife and natural resources depend. And while there is undoubtedly reason to point the finger at commercial corporations, big business isn't alone in its culpability. Even conservation charities sometimes contribute to the problems they purport to fight: I have heard first hand how the actions and subsequent inactions of one led to an increase in poaching and illegal logging in Africa (see pages 96–97). Observations elsewhere on my travels reveal that this is not an isolated incident.

Between the animals and the authorities are the people, villagers trying to eek a subsistence living out

◀ *Art Wolfe, contributor to this book, is a hugely talented and prolific photographer of the natural world, and a passionate advocate of wildlife conservation.*

of inadequate resources; who are themselves living on the edge. It is these people who have most amazed me, through their tolerance, their optimism, their ideas and their hopes for the future. In the developed world, it is easy to talk about conservation and even to get involved. We have money in our pockets and time on our hands. But if you are living in abject poverty, your children starving, your home a mud and stick hut, conservation is a luxury. And even in the developed world, when hard times strike, conservation swiftly suffers. In the aftermath of the global economic crisis of 2008, when tens of thousands of people lost their jobs, the value of savings and pensions collapsed, and house prices crashed to values lower than the mortgages owed on them – when we faced our own version of poverty – contributions to charities fell by over US$500 million. It was not that

◀ *The photographs in this book would never have happened without the help of a great many people who lent their skills and effort, such as my team of 'Buffalo Soldiers' in Nepal.*

people lost sympathy with charitable causes; it was simply that they no longer felt able to fund them.

Yet in the developing world, even among those who have nothing, the overwhelming impression I have gained from my time in the field is that the majority of people would work hard to support their natural resources. Even those who illegally harvest natural resources more often than not take such actions as a matter of last resort – a last-ditch step between survival and starvation.

▶ In the developing world, with its extremes of poverty, conservation is a luxury that few can afford.

Unfortunately this is rarely grasped by people in the developed world, where a thriving populist media, more interested in sentimental simplifications than complex realities, is largely responsible for the misconceptions held by many people, particularly in the West.

This was borne out by an encounter in India with a group of super wealthy Western businessmen on safari. One of them took an interest in my work and we fell into conversation. I explained that I was looking to interview tiger poachers so that I could understand their motives.

'What's there to understand? It's simple,' the man asserted. 'It all comes down to a five letter word – g-r-e-e-d. Poachers are simply greedy.'

I'm unsure whether this individual, who by his own admission had spent the best part of his working life pursuing the accumulation of more wealth than he would need in several lifetimes, saw the irony in his observation, but, more importantly, his views showed a grave lack of understanding of the realities faced by people inhabiting countries less wealthy than our own. He is not alone in his opinion, and I don't mean to judge him for it: such notions are the easy fictions of our times.

But for those prepared to delve behind the media rhetoric, as I have done during the course of this project, it becomes increasingly apparent that there is always more than one side to the story. I am no apologist for poachers. I abhor what they do. But I have talked with them and listened to their experiences, in an effort to comprehend their actions (see pages 152–53). I responded to the

businessman by explaining that a tiger poacher earns between US$7 and $15 for a pelt – hardly a lavish amount – and went on to describe the conditions in which most poachers live, and the literal life-and-death struggles they face each day. I also recounted the story of Matunde and explained how a revolutionary approach to conservation by an American businessman, Mike Korchinsky, had effectively solved the problem of human/elephant conflict in the region. By combining protection of wilderness habitats with local job-creation, school- and factory-building, Korchinsky's Wildlife Works company radically changed the way the local community views its natural resources. Wildlife became to them an asset worth much more alive than dead.

As he listened, I could see the man's opinion beginning to change. And herein lies the purpose of this book. It is my belief that a solid foundation for a sustainable action plan for wildlife conservation is only possible once we truly grasp the issues facing the people who coexist with the animals we seek to protect. If we can educate the men and women who have the power and wherewithal to instigate change, if we can show them a better way, it may just be possible to modify the behaviour of the people living on the frontline – the place where policies translate into effective results.

I am not alone in this view. A 2008 report by Johann Eliasch, the UK's special representative on deforestation and clean energy, and commissioned by UK Prime Minister Gordon Brown, stated that: 'Deforestation will continue as long as cutting down trees is more economic than preserving them.' He's right. Frances Seymour of the Centre for International Forestry Research, an international research and global knowledge institution committed to conserving forests and improving people's livelihoods, was equally blunt in a 2008 *National Geographic* article about Borneo's rainforests: 'Let's be clear here: Why do people cut down trees? For the money. If you give people the opportunity to make the same amount of money or more by leaving the trees standing, there's your answer.'

Fortunately, there are people who not only agree, but who are developing ideas and strategies to bring this about. People such as Mike Korchinsky, or Eric Kimmel, designer and founder of America's Rich Hippie boutique, who is pioneering a commercial fashion industry in Sierra Leone, West Africa, to bring work and hope to that country's people. Or others such as Hylton M. Philipson and Andrew Mitchell, Managing Director and Executive Director respectively of Canopy Capital, a London-based investment company that is attempting to give financial value to the services rainforests provide – services such as rainfall generation, moderation of extreme weather, carbon storage and biodiversity maintenance. 'Putting a price on these services,' says Canopy, 'is like taking out an insurance policy to maintain our life support system and has the potential to generate billions of dollars for forest-owning nations.'

Marrying capitalism with conservation may be the only realistic way forward in the fight against extinction. There is no doubt that we live in a world driven by economics, as was underlined by a recent case involving Donald Trump. The US tycoon wanted to develop a US\$1 billion golf resort near the town of Balmedie on the east coast of Scotland. The area the resort was to be sited includes an extensive system of sand dunes, a designated Site of Special Scientific Interest stretching for 22 kilometres (14 miles)

and supporting a vast array of plant and animal life. After due consideration of the plans, the local authority, Aberdeenshire Council, denied the planning application. Unhappy with the verdict, ministers of the Scottish parliament called in the application, effectively taking the decision out of local hands. Furthermore, councillor Martin Ford, who had used his casting vote to reject the original application, was sacked from his post as chairman of the council's Infrastructure Services Committee. Scottish Finance Secretary John Swinney subsequently approved the application at national level. Commenting on the case, First Minister of Scotland Alex Salmond stated: 'The economic benefits substantially outweigh any environmental impact.'

Whether or not one agrees with the decision to approve the development (and many do), the message is clear: a nation's economy is more important than its wildlife. This attitude is not exclusive to Scotland, nor indeed to the developed world – it's an attitude common to every government of every country in the world. Make no mistake: the principal reason that Rwanda's gorilla conservation programme is so successful is the fact that gorilla tourism is the country's third-highest earner of foreign revenue.

If anyone doubts the precedence the economy takes over all else we have only to look at the events of October 2008 and the global financial crisis. Within a matter of days, the United States had approved US\$700 billion of funding for its banking sector, a figure almost double

◀ *A Google Earth satellite image showing part of the system of sand dunes near Balmedie, Scotland, a Site of Special Scientific Interest and soon to be the location of a billion-dollar golf development.*

▶ *Mountain gorillas in Rwanda have benefited from a very effective conservation campaign supported by a forward-looking government (see pages 84–85).*

the country's existing budget deficit. In a similarly short space of time, the UK agreed to make £400 billion of new money available to its banks, and the Managing Director of the International Monetary Fund pledged to make 'hundreds of millions of dollars' available in an effort to avert further damage to the global economy. If just 1% of that money and a fraction of the urgency shown by the governments involved were to be directed towards solving our environmental crisis, the world would be a far safer haven for its wildlife – and for us.

Einstein once said that the definition of insanity is doing the same thing again and again and expecting a different result. In the field of conservation, it is time to accept that many of the old ways aren't working nearly well enough. For example, between 1998 and 2005 it is estimated that international donors spent over US$41 million on wild tiger conservation projects. Despite that, an official government census revealed that India's wild tiger population had declined to around 1,411 individuals in early 2008, down from 3,642 in 2002. Tiger conservation in India isn't working, and it is far from unique. We need to look at the problem differently – we need a better way.

Mel White is a frequent contributor to *National Geographic* magazine. In a November 2008 article about the threats to biodiversity in Borneo, he described a dream. I shall quote him at length, for although his narrative is specific to Borneo, its principles apply across all the regions I have visited:

'Along a dirt road in southern Borneo stands a one-room wooden house, with a few banana trees in the yard and a small vegetable garden in back. Beside the house a man kneels, washing a Yamaha Jupiter Z motorbike. It's red, and it shines in the hot sun as the man rinses off the soap.

'The man's name is, let's say, Pak Wang. With his new motorbike he can go to the closest village in a few minutes, instead of walking nearly an hour along the road. In the village he can meet his friends, buy things, go to the little karaoke bar, and watch television in his uncle's restaurant. He can feel part of the world.

'Pak Wang wants a mobile phone. Most of his friends have one, and if he had one it would be easier for him to make plans with them, to know where they will be on Sunday night, to meet the pretty woman named Unita who sells fruit at a street stand in town.'

White continues: 'So. Here is a message to the world. If we want to protect the forests of Borneo, to preserve a substantial part of its stupendous biodiversity, to make sure that orangutans have places to build their nightly nests and hornbills have fruit to eat and flying frogs have trees to live in, there's only one way to do it. We need to find a way for Pak Wang to buy his mobile phone. And, after he marries the pretty fruit seller, a way for them to keep their children healthy and send them to school. A way that offers them a better future without having to turn their forests into plantations of oil palm or the sterile pits of strip mines.

'And we need to do it while there's still something left to protect.'

These are my sentiments exactly.

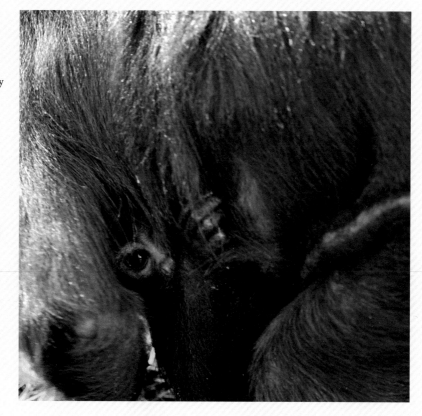

◀ *A baby black-headed spider monkey peeps out as it clings to its mother. If this and many other Critically Endangered species are to survive, we need to find 21st-century solutions to the challenge of conservation.*

THE AMERICAS

Constituting the ecologically diverse regions of North, Central and South America, the Americas are home to 228 – over a quarter – of the world's most endangered terrestrial mammal species. Notable among them are several species of primate, including the brown spider monkey, Panamanian spider monkey, and golden lion and golden-headed lion tamarins; several cat species, including two species of panther (the Florida panther and eastern panther), Andean mountain cat and Texas ocelot; three species of otter (sea otter, marine otter and giant otter); and the last remaining population of red wolves.

The vast majority of endangered mammal species across this region – 200 out of 228 – are concentrated in South and Central America. The bias towards these regions is unsurprising, given that Central America was until recently entirely covered with rainforest, and the Amazon region in South America is home to the world's largest tropical rainforest and a tenth of all mammal species.

Loss of habitat due to deforestation is a major issue in conservation across all the areas covered in this book, and it is the single biggest threat to wildlife in Central and South America, where over half of endangered or critically endangered terrestrial mammal species are found in forest habitat.

The remaining endangered species across all three regions reside largely in shrublands or grasslands (26% overall), with a similar number in South America inhabiting areas of savannah or wetland habitats. Many of the latter are endemic to the Pantanal in Brazil, the world's largest freshwater wetland system. In Central America, desert dwellers form the second largest group of endangered species.

In South America, deforestation and development of land for agriculture are the predominant threats to endangered mammals, followed by trade in forest products (biological resource use) and other, non-agricultural forms of land development. In Central America, deforestation for resource use is highest on the list of threats to mammals, followed by the threat posed by invasive species.

In North America the threats are more diverse, but agricultural and other development there affect over three-quarters of endangered species. And, as in Central America, invasive species are also having a detrimental impact on native mammals.

Climate change currently poses the least direct threat to species in these regions, affecting only around 6% of threatened mammals. Also figuring relatively low on the list of threats are pollution and industries such as mining.

What these figures emphatically indicate is that deforestation, whether for resource use (such as harvesting of timber), for agricultural development or for other human needs, is the greatest threat to mammals in the Americas, a region supporting some of the world's most important forests and the second highest number of endangered mammals of the five zones covered in this book.

FLORIDA PANTHER (PUMA, COUGAR)

Puma concolor coryi
Critically endangered

Pumas have the largest range of any terrestrial mammal in the western hemisphere, extending from Canada to southern Chile. They were eliminated from eastern North America within 200 years of European colonization. However, a remnant, isolated sub-population numbering 70–80 individuals persists in Florida. Pumas are threatened by loss and fragmentation of their habitat, and by poaching of their prey base. They are also subject to retaliatory hunting due to the threat they pose to livestock and on occasion to human life. There is a need for the implementation of programmes to reduce conflict arising from livestock depredation.

▶ *A Florida panther sits in the dense understorey vegetation that is its preferred environment.*

RED WOLF

Canis rufus
Critically endangered

Red wolves were extinct in
the wild until the US Fish
& Wildlife Service began a
reintroduction programme in
eastern North Carolina in 1987.
The total existing population
now numbers fewer than 150,
of which no more than 50
are mature individuals. The
current primary threat to the
species' survival in the wild is
hybridization with coyotes, a
factor in their initial demise.

◀   *A red wolf patrols the
    pack's territory in North
    Carolina, USA.*

INDIANA BAT

Myotis sodalis
Endangered

The population of Indiana bats has declined by over 50% in the past decade. Historically the species' range covered the midwestern, south central and northeastern US, but the species has now disappeared or greatly declined in most of the northeast. Human disturbance at winter caves, exacerbated by the commercialization of cave systems for tourism, is a significant threat, since arousal during hibernation causes depletion of the bats' energy reserves. To help conserve the species, maternity roosts need protecting and suitable summer habitat must be made available through sympathetic forest management.

▶ *A roost of Indiana bats in south central United States.*

BLACK-HEADED SPIDER MONKEY

Ateles fusciceps
Critically endangered

There are two recognized subspecies of *Ateles fusciceps*, one endemic to Ecuador, the other found in Colombia and Panama. In Ecuador, the population is poorly distributed, highly fragmented, and has declined by *c.* 80%, due primarily to habitat loss and hunting. The story is similar in Colombia. As well as increasing the size of protected areas and instigating an ex-situ breeding programme, there is a need to promote conservation awareness among local communities, in particular the threat posed by primate trafficking. Conservationists also need to deepen their understanding of the factors contributing to ongoing deforestation and hunting.

▶ *In the wild, black-headed spider monkeys are usually seen alone or in small groups of 2–4 individuals.*

▶▶ *The only persistent bond between individuals is that of a mother and her offspring.*

GEOFFROY'S SPIDER MONKEY

Ateles geoffroyi
Endangered

Spider monkeys travel and forage in the upper levels of their forest habitat. They spend much of their time in the canopy and also use the middle and lower strata, but are rarely seen in the understorey. The major threat to the species is habitat loss, with a number of subspecies, including the Geoffroy's spider monkey, having been subject to very high rates of loss. However, there remain several large areas of relatively continuous habitat in the Selva Maya forest region that extends across Belize, Guatemala and Mexico; in Nicaragua and Honduras; and in Panama's Darien jungle. The species is subject to exploitation by pet traffickers and is hunted in some regions.

▶ *Spider monkeys spend a lot of time hanging from branches and rarely venture down to ground level.*

▶▶ *Spider monkeys live in groups of up to 20–30 individuals. Each female has a 'core area' of the group's home range which she uses most.*

▶▶ *Overleaf: Mother and baby share a close bond, but individuals are otherwise rarely seen together.*

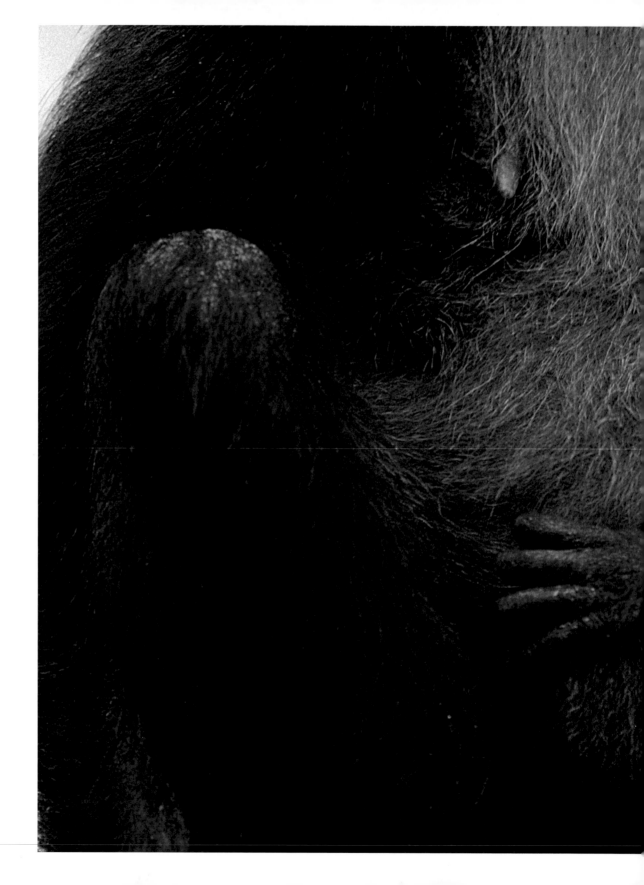

YUCATAN BLACK HOWLER MONKEY

Alouatta pigra
Endangered

Howler monkeys are the large leaf-eaters of the South American primate communities. Their most characteristic feature is their deep jaw, which accommodates an enlarged larynx and hyoid apparatus or resonating chamber. It is with this highly specialized voice box that the howler monkey produces the howls (grunts, roars and barks) from which it gets its name. Howling sessions, usually involving the entire group, can be heard particularly in the early morning and are audible at distances of up to two kilometres. The main threats to this species are deforestation, hunting for food and for the pet trade, and disease, in particular yellow fever epidemics.

◄ Howler monkeys spend up to three-quarters of their day lying quietly among the branches, fermenting leaves in a specially adapted caecum, part of the digestive tract.

ON THE FRONTLINE:
BRAZIL

▶ *The Amazon rainforest
supports a population
of 25 million people.*

John Carter feels let down. Badly. John is an American who 12 years ago moved to the Amazon region with his Brazilian wife. He had grown up with campaigns to save the rainforest and, like many people, had assumed the international NGOs were getting the job done.

'I had a tremendous let-down,' he says passionately. 'I thought they were doing a whole lot more. I thought from all the rhetoric you hear in the media, etc, that there'd been a real, huge impact on conservation and I then came here and saw it was absolutely the contrary.'

The facts back John up. During two decades of earnest campaigning to save rainforests, the world has lost 20% of the Amazon to development. Several species of primate, as well as other mammals, are on the verge of extinction. And in recent years the speed of destruction has increased: the first five years of the 21st century saw the same amount of deforestation as the whole of the last decade of the 20th century (Brazilian National Institute of Space Research/UN Food and Agriculture Organization).

Perhaps part of the reason for this disparity is the failure to grasp that the Amazon region is home not just to an extraordinary diversity of flora and fauna, but to a human population. This is the view of Roberto Unger, Minister for Strategic Affairs in the Brazilian government: 'The world often fails to understand that the Amazon is not just a collection of trees, it is a group of people. More than 25 million people live and work in the Amazon. It is 60% of our national territory. If the communities who live there lack economic alternatives that are compatible with preservation of the rainforests, they will be inexorably driven to deforestation.'

The export revenue generated in Brazil by timber products is around US$500 million (excluding paper products). But this figure is dwarfed by the value of Brazil's soybean and beef industries, which amount to US$10 billion and US$4 billion respectively. Soybeans and their derivatives are Brazil's largest export earner, and the country has overtaken Australia to become the world's leading producer of beef. Most Brazilian soybeans and cattle are farmed on cleared Amazonian land.

The people in power in Brazil are largely on the side of the developers. Blairo Maggi is Governor of Mato Grosso, the most heavily deforested area of the Amazon. He is forthright in his views: 'It is not possible to develop a country economically without using its natural resources. We have no computer industry and little manufacturing. We have a lot of land. It should be used for the Brazilian people. If someone thinks that the Amazon is the lungs of the earth then they need to pay Brazil for that service. There is no other way.'

And it seems there is a way richer nations can help. John Carter, disillusioned at the NGOs' lack of impact, formed the Land Alliance in an effort to bring sustainable development to the heart of the Amazon. Part of that plan was for farmers to protect enough of the forest to offset their own emissions. Going a step further, farmers could then sell surplus carbon credits to businesses internationally, gaining additional revenue from their forested land. Rabobank, a Dutch bank focusing on the food and agribusiness sectors, approached the Land Alliance to help with offsetting its carbon emissions. Under the terms of their agreement, Rabobank pays the Alliance a sum for each tonne of carbon offset. The deal means farmers make three times as much per hectare by letting the forest grow than they could by clearing the land to rear cattle, or twice what they could earn from growing soybeans. The 1.6 million hectares of land certified by the

◄ *The first five years of the 21st century saw more logging in the Amazon than the last ten years of the 20th century.*

Land Alliance are now worth more with trees standing than they would be if the trees were cleared.

It is an idea that is catching on. In February 2009, the UK Conservative Party announced that it is to offset its carbon emissions by backing a similar initiative, the Juma Project, brainchild of Professor Virgilio Viana, former Environment Secretary for Amazonas. While in office Viana created several protected areas, reducing rates of deforestation in the state by two-thirds. He recognized, however, that other strategies were needed to protect the forest in the long term. 'You've got to look at why people deforest,' he explains. 'It's not because they are stupid, irrational or hate forest. Most forest dwellers are very poor. If I was living in a shack like theirs, I'd sell a mahogany tree for ten bucks to get milk for my children.'

The Juma Project pays the Boa Frente community a monthly income in return for zero deforestation and a commitment to send children to school. The community has been given a solar panel and a computer and further investment to fund social programmes and health clinics. The project is monitored using satellite imagery.

Both the Juma Project and the Land Alliance are founded on a simple premise summed up succinctly by John Carter: 'If you place an economic value on the Amazon, all of a sudden people want to protect it.'

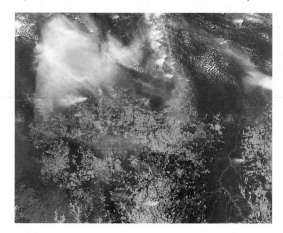

◄ *A NASA satellite photograph showing deforestation in the Brazilian state of Mato Grosso.*

GOLDEN LION TAMARIN

Leontopithecus rosalia
Endangered

The golden lion tamarin is a small monkey inhabiting a severely fragmented range of less than 5,000 km² (2,000 miles²) in the state of Rio de Janeiro, one of the most densely populated regions of Brazil. The quality of its habitat and area of occupancy both continue to decline. Conservation work to augment wild populations with captive-bred individuals has had some success, but there remain numerous threats to the wild population and much depends on the continuing efforts of organizations such as the International Committee for the Conservation of Lion Tamarins, set up by the Brazilian Government in 1990.

▶ *A golden lion tamarin emerges from a tree hole, used as a sleeping site.*

▶▶ *An adaptable mammal, the tamarin's main need is for sufficient food sources and foraging sites.*

BLACK LION TAMARIN

Leontopithecus chrysopygus
Endangered

This species is now highly
fragmented, occurring in
only 11 isolated populations
in Brazil's São Paulo state.
Only one of these groups,
in Morro do Diabo State Park,
is considered to be viable in
the long term. Inbreeding
depression due to the isolation
and small size of existing
populations is being addressed
through meta-population
management, for example
the translocation of animals
from one breeding group to
another, and the introduction
of captive-bred animals.
Other conservation efforts
are focusing on education
work in local communities,
the preservation of remaining
forest fragments, and the
creation of forest corridors
to establish areas of
continuous habitat.

▶ *Lion tamarins are an
adaptable species well
able to live in degraded
and secondary forests,
depending only on
sufficient year-round food
sources and tree holes that
they use as sleeping sites.*

GOLDEN-HEADED LION TAMARIN

Leontopithecus chrysomelas
Endangered

The golden-headed lion tamarin still occurs in over a hundred localities in the Brazilian state of Bahia. However, these surviving populations are seriously depleted and fragmented, as the state's remaining forests are being destroyed at an unprecedented rate due to the decline in the cocoa industry and the consequential expansion of the palm oil and coconut industries. One factor in the species' survival to date is thought to be the traditional 'cabruca' system for shading cacao trees, whereby some of the original canopy trees are left standing, so providing a connection between forest patches. Properly managed, this could be an important tool in future conservation efforts.

◄　*Tamarins eat fruits, flowers, nectar, plant gums and animal prey, including frogs, snails, lizards, spiders and insects.*

▶▶　*Overleaf: Their long fingers and hands enable them to forage effectively for prey.*

COTTON-HEADED TAMARIN

Saguinus oedipus
Critically endangered

The cotton-headed tamarin occurs in northwestern Colombia, in an area of intensive human colonization and forest loss. An estimated 75% of the species' original habitat has been cleared for agriculture and pasture; what remains consists predominantly of small, isolated forest patches. Further habitat loss will result from the planned construction of a hydroelectric dam, which is expected to flood more than 500 km² (200 miles²) of forest within the species' last major stronghold. Conservation efforts include educational campaigns and an agricultural training programme to decrease pressure on the forest by local communities.

▶ *Tamarins live in extended family groups of as many as 15 individuals, but more usually in smaller groups of 2–8.*

▶▶ *Tamarins are distinguished from the other monkeys of the New World by their small size and modified claws.*

ON THE FRONTLINE:
GUYANA

Bharrat Jagdeo is the President of Guyana. He is unusual among world leaders in that not only does he talk about halting climate change, he is actually trying to do something immediate to achieve it.

Guyana, a small country on the northern coast of South America sandwiched between Brazil, Venezuela and Suriname, is host to 200,000 km² (80,000 miles²) of rainforest. The Kyoto Protocol provides financial incentives to those who replant after cutting down trees, but there is no reward for leaving ancient forest intact. The government of Guyana is therefore under mounting pressure to allow logging and development of its forest in order to boost the country's under-developed economy.

Instead, President Jagdeo wants to protect Guyana's rainforests and the wildlife that inhabits them. And so in 2007 he wrote a letter to UK Prime Minister Gordon Brown offering to place Guyana's entire standing forest under the control of a British-led international body in return for a bilateral deal with the UK that would secure development aid and the technical assistance needed for Guyana to make the change to a green economy.

It took the UK government a year to reply. When it did the answer was, essentially, thanks but no thanks. An official response, delivered in September 2008, stated that: 'Rather than dealing separately with individual cases an overall international approach is needed to reduce deforestation significantly.' It went on: 'reduced emissions from deforestation and degradation should be part of a post-2012 climate deal.'

In other words, rather than take immediate and productive action, they would rather prevaricate for another four years before getting a committee together to talk some more. Meantime, at the current rate of deforestation, another 600 km² (230 miles²) of Guyana's rainforest will be irrevocably destroyed, and that is assuming President Jagdeo can hold off the logging companies and agribusinesses clamouring to get in. If he fails, the scale of deforestation will be much wider.

President Jagdeo admits he had 'hoped for a more aggressive response'. Undaunted, he continues to look for other solutions, citing the emissions trading scheme in Europe, which developed from nothing into a US$33 billion industry in just two years, as inspiration for how his own country's economy could benefit from capitalism without compromising its environment.

And, where the UK government failed, London's money markets may yet step in. Hylton M. Philipson is the Managing Director of Canopy Capital founded in 2007, a company that has created an investment template for 'first-movers' in the ecosystem services market. Philipson asserts: 'Past efforts have not engaged the power of money and the markets, and these are things that are destroying the rainforest: the fact that you can make money out of beef or soya or palm oil [three of the main products from cleared forest land] but you can't make money out of a standing forest.'

'Think of the rainforest as a utility,' he continues, 'just like an energy or water company. It's providing rainfall, oxygen, maintaining biodiversity, and conserving carbon. Now, if you want these services you better start paying for them.'

Having to pay for our rainfall, oxygen and carbon storage may not prove popular. But why should rich, developed nations expect poor countries like Guyana (and others with vast swathes of rainforest, such as

▶ *A Google Earth satellite image and map showing the Iwokrama Forest, where conservationists are developing new, capitalist models for rainforest protection.*

Malaysia, Indonesia and the countries of central Africa) to subsidize our consumption of these 'services' just because they happen to own the 'factories' that produce them?

Canopy Capital's initial scheme involves the 4,000 km² (1,500 miles²) Iwokrama Forest in Guyana. This lies at the heart of the Guiana Shield, an area of rainforest covering much of Guyana, Suriname and French Guiana, as well as parts of Colombia, Venezuela and Brazil, and boasting one of the richest biodiversities in the world. Dane Gobin of the Iwokrama International Centre for Rainforest Conservation and Development supports the initiative: 'Capitalism, if properly managed and directed and structured, could do it [prevent deforestation]. For a long time the international community and green movements have relied a lot on donations. We believe in investment and capital.'

Not surprisingly, some more traditional conservation groups disagree – Friends of the Earth, for one. Tom Pickens is their International Climate Campaigner and he questions the socio-economic benefits of capital-based solutions. 'Rich nations do need to support poorer nations,' he told me. 'The question is how?'

One answer is to pay compensation to both governments and companies that agree to refrain from deforestation. This way, the economic benefits of deforestation are not lost and a developing country can continue to grow its economy. Governments can use the income to fund social welfare programmes, while corporations can use it to diversify and maintain their investment in a nation's economy. But this is not a solution favoured by Friends of the Earth, who object to logging companies being compensated for not cutting down trees. Such an objection may seem logical ... except for the fact that it is not governments but companies that

◄ *President Bharrat Jagdeo of Guyana approached the UK government with a plan to help protect his country's rainforest. The UK declined.*

drive economic growth. By simply removing companies' ability to generate profits – profits that not only go to shareholders but are also invested in expansion, new jobs, better wages and improved working conditions – all that is achieved is economic decline when they close down or relocate. Of course money must only be handed out with great caution and tied to strict conditions. But big business must be included in the solutions to a region's problems if those solutions are to be at all effective in the long term.

For decades conservationists have been locked into conflict with big business. It is now time to make industry part of the solution, as is beginning to happen in Malaysia through organizations such as the Roundtable on Sustainable Palm Oil, a collaboration between grassroots groups, environmental and social NGOs, and companies involved in the palm oil sector.

Of course, some of the arguments of groups such as Friends of the Earth have merit. But as wiser people than me – President Jagdeo, Dane Gobin, Hylton M. Philipson, John Carter in Brazil – have pointed out, the traditional methods of conservation have failed. We need a new plan. If the developed world is to help countries such as Guyana transition to a sustainable economy and resist more destructive industries such as logging, and in so doing help to preserve the habitats of endangered species, then it has an obligation to ensure that the solutions it proposes deliver an equivalent level of long-term economic growth that will provide employment, housing and social development – not just a lump sum in aid.

GIANT OTTER

Pteronura brasiliensis
Endangered

The giant otter is the largest of the 13 otter species and is endemic to the rainforests and wetlands of South America. Illegal harvesting for pelts continues in some regions, but otters are also killed by logging and mining workers who blame otters for depleting local fish resources. Otters are also taken by indigenous groups for whom the meat and pelt are part of their traditional subsistence economy. There is recent evidence that contaminants such as mercury from gold mines are further depleting numbers, as are introduced diseases such as canine distemper and parvovirus. For conservation efforts to be effective, conflicts with subsistence and commercial fishermen must be addressed.

▶ *The preferred fish diet of the giant otter includes members of the catfish, perch and characin families. When fish are less abundant, it feeds on crustaceans, small snakes and small caimans.*

EUROPE & NORTH ASIA

The region of Europe and northern Asia covers an enormous area of roughly 27 million km² (10.5 million miles²) and includes territories both above and below the Arctic Circle, extending from the North Atlantic Ocean down to the Mediterranean Sea and across as far as the Russian Far East. Yet despite its scale and breadth, it is home to just 38 endangered terrestrial mammal species, or almost 5% of the global total.

Among those 38 species are some of the world's most critically endangered cats, including the Amur leopard, of which no more than 30 widely dispersed individuals remain in the wild; the Iberian lynx, which has a wild population of fewer than 150 adults; and one of the world's most iconic endangered species, the Amur or Siberian tiger.

Russia, whose huge territories extend across most of northern Asia, has the world's largest forest reserves and its greatest reserves of mineral and energy resources. Perhaps surprisingly, however, industrial activity and deforestation are not the predominant threats to the mammal species of northern Asia. In fact the single greatest threat is posed by alien species, affecting almost half of endangered mammals, whether through hybridization, predation, or competition for food sources. This is followed by human intrusion and redevelopment of land for agricultural use. Other serious threats include modification of natural ecosystems, pollution and global warming.

In Europe, the greatest threats are posed by a combination of invasive species, which affect almost half of endangered mammal species, and biological resource use, impacting an equivalent number. Redevelopment of land for agricultural use is the third greatest threat, affecting one third of endangered species. Pollution is also a significant threat in the region, impacting over a quarter of species.

Without one dominating habitat comparable with the rainforests of South America or Southeast Asia, endangered species are spread across a variety of habitat types, including grassland, shrubland, forest and desert.

Why is the overall number of endangered terrestrial mammals so low in comparison with other regions? The lack of tropical forest habitat may be one explanation: North Africa, also devoid of tropical forest, has a similarly low total. It may also be that the more developed nations of Europe, and to some extent Russia, are less economically dependent on forestry and the timber trade, and therefore have less of an incentive to permit unsustainable deforestation.

However, the figures are undoubtedly also skewed by the fact that many native mammal species were exterminated centuries ago. In the UK, for example, wolves, bears, lynx and, until recently, beavers have long been extinct in the wild. In this regard, less developed parts of the world are fortunate still to have the chance to save their natural heritage.

Conversely, the range of threats to endangered species is more diverse than in other regions. For example, providing total protection to the rainforests of South and Central America would secure over half of that region's endangered mammals. The same cannot be said of Europe and northern Asia, where immediate and effective protection of all forest habitat would secure the future of only a quarter of critically threatened species. Consequently, the conservation challenges in these regions demand a wider range of strategies and solutions.

AMUR (SIBERIAN) TIGER

Panthera tigris ssp. *altaica*
Endangered

The Amur tiger has made a spectacular comeback since the 1930s, when numbers fell to between 20 and 30 individuals. A recent census estimates the current population at 331–393 adult or sub-adult tigers, 90% of which belong to one sub-population in the Sikhote-Alin mountains of Russia's Far East. A second sub-population occurs along Russia's southernmost coast, cut off by the urban area of Vladivostok, but adjoining China's critically endangered population in the Changbai mountains. Overall, the Amur tiger population is considered stable. However, poaching, human/tiger conflict and prey base depletion continue, potentially threatening the species' hard-won gains.

◄ *A mane of fur around the neck and head, an adaptation against the cold, differentiates the Amur subspecies of tiger.*

►► *Overleaf and following pages: Amur tigers are well adapted to a harsh winter climate. Tigers' whiskers are used in navigation and hunting, and to communicate mood.*

IBERIAN LYNX

Lynx pardinus
Critically endangered

The Iberian lynx is perilously close to extinction. There are believed to be between just 84 and 143 left, living in isolated pockets of Spain and possibly Portugal, with insufficient adults for the species to survive. The downward trend is continuing due to severe depletion of their primary prey base (rabbits), disease, hunting, high unnatural mortality rates (especially road deaths), and habitat destruction and fragmentation. Education and awareness programmes, particularly among landowners, as well as captive breeding have begun in Spain. Moving forward, priority must be given to maintaining suitable habitat to accommodate expanded populations.

▶ *The lynx favours a mosaic of dense scrub for shelter, and open pasture for hunting rabbits.*

▶▶ *Overleaf, left: The tufts of hair on its ears enable the lynx to detect sound sources, greatly enhancing its hearing capacity.*

▶▶ *Overleaf, right: The Iberian lynx is a specialized feeder, with rabbits accounting for 80–100% of its diet.*

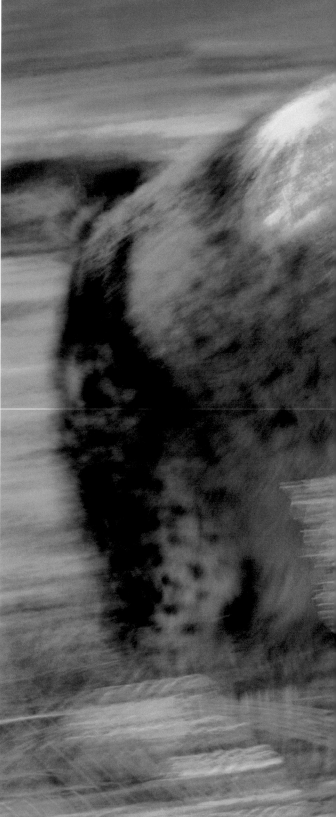

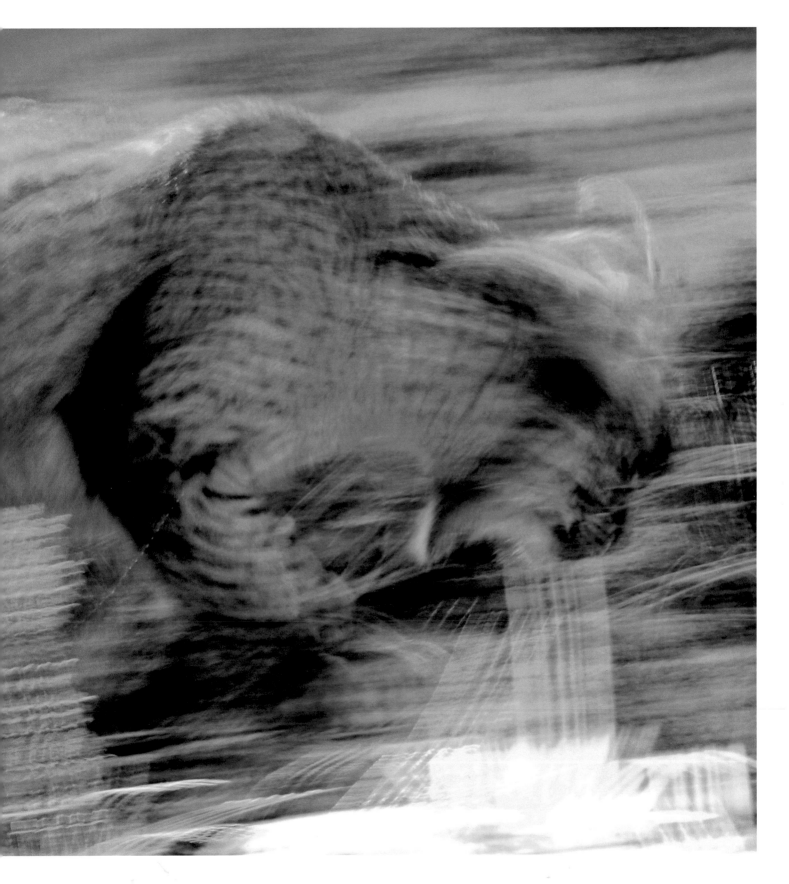

ON THE FRONTLINE:
PORTUGAL

To the east of the capital city of Lisbon and stretching across 25,000 km² (10,000 miles²) of southern Portugal, as far as the hills of the Spanish border, lies the region of Alentejo, an area of outstanding natural beauty that supports a multitude of wildlife species, many of them endangered or unique to the region. They include over a hundred species of bird, numerous amphibians, bats, and one of the world's most endangered big cats – the Iberian lynx. It is one of the most important natural habitats in Western Europe. And it is under threat.

Alentejo is the centre of a multi-billion dollar international agricultural industry – the cork industry. This is worth around US$2 billion annually and creates employment for upwards of 60,000 workers. Surprisingly, however, it is not what is threatening the region's wildlife. Quite the opposite: centuries of agricultural tradition are responsible for creating the rich tapestry of habitat that benefits such a diversity of species. This manmade agricultural ecosystem, known as the

▶ *Intensive farming is increasing the pressure on natural habitats and wildlife in the Iberian Peninsula.*

Montado, combines scattered tree cover with pasture, and has been carefully created and managed by farmers for centuries.

Industrial-scale cultivation and harvesting of cork in the Montado dates back to the 18th century, although cork has been harvested here for more than two millennia. An average tree, which can be harvested once every nine years, yields enough cork to produce 4,000 bottle stoppers, the principal use of this natural material. Harvesting is still done by hand by skilled workers using *machados* (curved axes), as no suitable mechanical means of stripping the trees' bark has yet been invented. Once harvested, the cork is transported to storage yards and on to factories that manufacture cork products.

In addition to providing a livelihood to the people of Alentejo – one of the poorest regions of Western Europe – and a home to an abundance of wildlife, the cork forests of the Montado absorb millions of tonnes of carbon dioxide each year, helping to combat global warming. Indeed, cork production is about as 'green' as any industry can be, so why are the wildlife of the Montado and the livelihoods of the inhabitants of Alentejo threatened? Like most things, the fate of the Montado is determined by economics. In the 1980s, the European Union (EU) incentivized Europe's farmers, by way of subsidies, to switch to more intensive crops such as maize. Lured by cash handouts, many complied. But the Alentejo region is susceptible to drought and its soil poorly suited to such crops. The policy created far more problems than it solved.

Around the same time that the EU was paying farmers to grow more intensive crops, consumption of wine increased dramatically and demand for cork stoppers grew exponentially. Struggling to keep up with increased demand, some factories allowed quality control to slip. As a result, there was an increase in the number of bottles of wine that became tainted by trichloroanisole (TCA) in corks. Unhappy that their wine was being spoiled, and driven by customer demand for more consistent quality, wine producers sought alternatives to cork, turning first to synthetic stoppers and, later, metal screw caps. These modern products are marketed

◄ *A 2002 survey using tracking, camera trapping and box trapping failed to detect a single Iberian lynx in Portugal – a sign that the species is close to extinction in the country.*

as being cleaner than cork, and wineries saw a decrease in tainted product of around 50%.

The cork industry rose to the challenge, launching a US$1 million research programme and introducing new systems of quality control that made cork stoppers cleaner and more reliable. In the meantime, however, the new competitors had taken 25% of the market and, having made their mark, are pushing to increase that share. As a result, demand for traditional cork stoppers has decreased, making it harder for the farmers of the Alentejo to sustain the industry and continue to make a living from the Montado. If the trend towards synthetic and metal cap stoppers continues then the likelihood is that the cork oaks and pastures will be cleared in favour of more profitable crops that inevitably will be less friendly to wildlife and the environment.

So what's the solution? By choosing to buy only wine with a cork stopper, the public can put pressure on retailers to demand traditional cork from the wineries. There are precedents for such consumer-driven campaigns, the most successful being the Fair Trade movement. However, even after decades of campaigning

and development, Fair Trade products account for a very small percentage of global sales. The farmers of Alentejo don't have that long.

A more immediate solution may lie in carbon trading. The ability of Portugal's cork oaks to absorb around 4.8 million tonnes of carbon dioxide a year is a valuable asset that has yet to be capitalized by the region's farmers. The current laws controlling carbon trading are complex. The European Clean Development Mechanism enables companies to invest in projects in developing countries that will lead to reduced emissions of greenhouse gases, instead of making difficult and expensive cuts to their own emissions. Under the restrictive terms of the Kyoto Protocol, this is not currently applicable in Alentejo; but that need not mean carbon trading cannot be a part of a future solution. Current regulations do reward landowners for replanting trees, which might allow for the restitution of cork forest cleared in the 1980s. But – as always – the priority must be to find a way for it to make economic sense for farmers to leave existing trees standing. Only then can the wildlife-rich forests of Alentejo be preserved to the benefit of both people and animals.

AMUR LEOPARD

Panthera pardus orientalis
Critically endangered

The Amur leopard is a very rare subspecies, with a 2007 census counting only 14–20 adults and 5–6 cubs in Primorsky Krai, at the southernmost tip of Russia's Far Eastern region. It is extinct in China and the Korean Peninsula. The species faces numerous threats, including encroaching civilization, road-building, poaching, commercial exploitation of forests and climate change. Numbers have fluctuated over recent years but the overall trend is downwards. The species' total range is estimated at just 2,500 km² (1,000 miles²).

◀ *A recent census counted only 14–20 adults and 5–6 cubs remaining in the wild.*

◀◀ *The Amur leopard has the lowest level of genetic variation of any leopard subspecies.*

TATRA CHAMOIS

Rupicapra rupicapra tatrica
Critically endangered

Occurring in the Tatra
Mountains of Poland and
Slovakia, the population of
Tatra chamois is thought to
be fewer than 200 individuals
and declining. Among its
major threats are poaching,
exacerbated in recent
times by an increase in the
availability of firearms; human
disturbance, particularly
from increased leisure and
tourism activity (an estimated
3 million people visit the Tatra
National Park each year); and
the deliberate introduction
of subspecies from diverse
geographic regions, leading
to hybridization. If the Tatra
chamois is to be saved, there
must be a reduction in illegal
hunting and the removal of
non-native introductions.

◄   *The population of Tatra
    chamois has been decreasing
    steadily since the 1960s.*

▶▶ *Overleaf: Chamois inhabit
    steep, rocky mountain areas.*

EUROPEAN BISON (LOWLAND-CAUCASIAN LINE)

Bison bonasus bonasus
Endangered

The European bison became extinct in the wild shortly after World War I. However, captive breeding programmes and intensive conservation efforts have revived the population of free-ranging bison to around 1,800 individuals. Of these, the Lowland-Caucasian line forms a declining population of just over 700. Conflict and political instability threaten the species in the Caucasus, where herds have suffered severe losses in recent years. Other threats include lack of habitat, population fragmentation, disease, hybridization and poaching. Europe's contemporary ecosystems and human population density leave little space for a large herbivore and limit the potential for a significant increase in bison numbers.

▶ *Historically widespread and numerous, the European bison has recovered from extinction in the wild, but remains threatened.*

▶▶ *Overleaf: European bison occur in habitat ranging from sea level to 2,100 m (7,000 ft) in the Caucasus.*

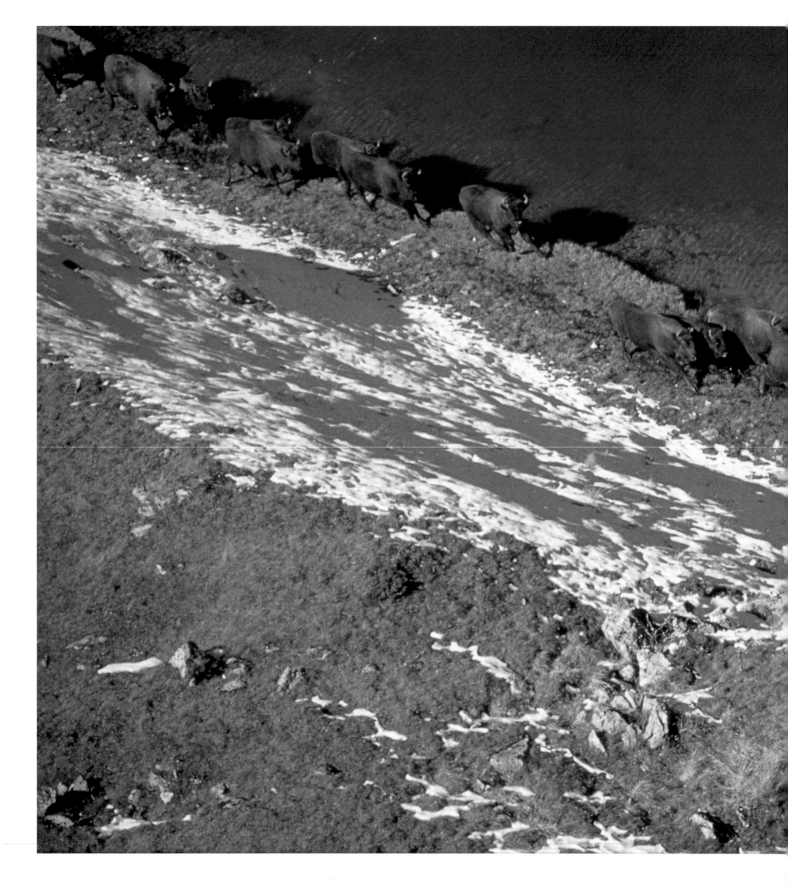

SEA OTTER

Enhydra lutris
Endangered

Sea otters inhabit a variety of near-shore marine environments and are generally found in areas protected from the most severe ocean winds, such as rocky coastlines and thick kelp forests. There are stable populations in coastal areas of far eastern Russia as well as in Alaska and at points along the Pacific coast of North America. However, heavy shipping means oil spills pose the greatest manmade threat to the species. Estimates of sea otter deaths following the 1989 *Exxon Valdez* spill ranged from 2,650 to 3,905. Commercial fishing also poses a threat, since otters are often caught in gill and trammel nets, causing them to drown.

▶ *Kelp forest is an important habitat component, used for foraging and resting.*

▶▶ *Overleaf: Sea otters typically stay within a kilometre of the shore.*

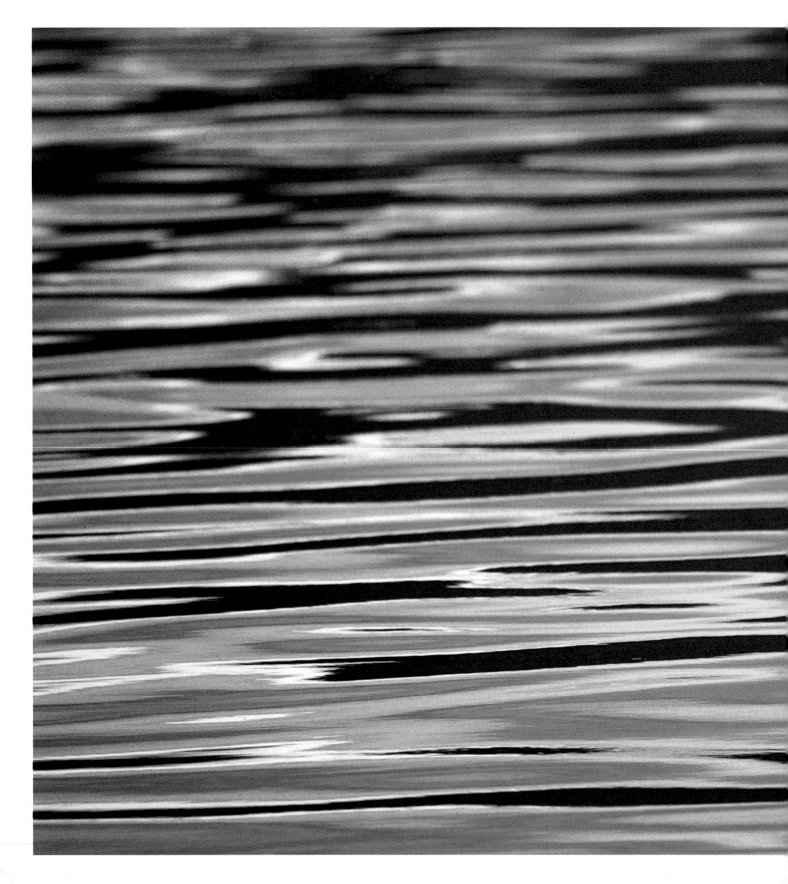

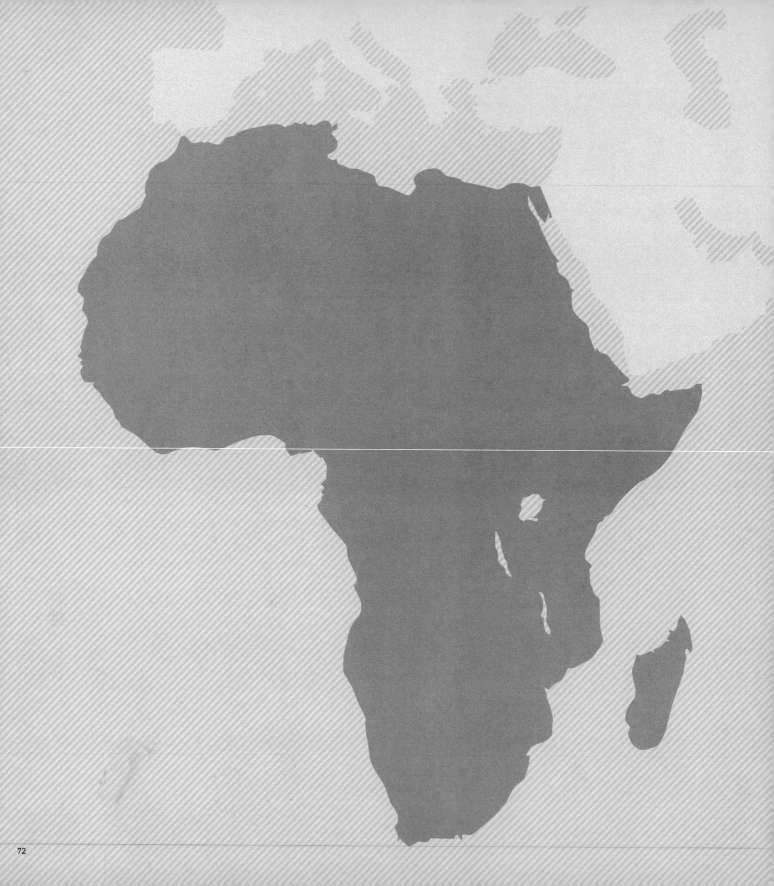

AFRICA

Africa boasts the world's greatest density, geographic range and diversity of wild animal populations, from large carnivores to mass concentrations of herbivores. The continent also contains its share of endangered terrestrial mammals – 158 species, representing almost 20% of the total. Among them are some of the planet's most iconic species, including mountain and lowland gorillas, chimpanzees, subspecies of leopard and cheetah, black rhinoceroses and painted hunting dogs.

Over 90% of the continent's endangered species inhabit sub-Saharan Africa. As with South and Central America, this bias is undoubtedly explained by habitat. Vast swathes of deciduous and semi-deciduous broadleaf forest and lowland evergreen rainforest provide a home to a huge diversity of fauna and flora. By contrast, the arid deserts of the continent's north are substantially less hospitable to wildlife and human life alike.

With such a large area of Africa covered by forest of one type or another – there are around 14 different forest ecosystems in Africa – it is little wonder that a large proportion of endangered mammals – over 70% – are found in forest habitats. Similarly, with high levels of human poverty and growing human population density across the region, it is no surprise that redevelopment of forest areas for agricultural use and the harvesting

of biological resources pose the greatest threats, affecting 122 (77%) and 97 (61%) endangered species respectively. Land development for human use and modification of natural systems pose the next greatest risks to mammals in sub-Saharan Africa. In North Africa the threats are more evenly distributed between a range of factors, including development and redevelopment of land, human intrusion, invasive species and global warming.

Poverty in Africa is chronic and rising. In 2009, 33 of the 49 nations on the United Nations list of Least Developed Countries were in Africa. Unemployment is higher than in any other developing region, running at up to 39% in parts of southern Africa (excluding Zimbabwe, where exceptional circumstances have caused unemployment to rise to over 90%). And, for those people in employment, an estimated 110 million are working for less than US$1 a day, unable to support their families or afford decent living conditions. Indeed, in many nations the average income for a working adult is less than US$1 a day.

Poor people make for poor conservationists: when your children are starving conservation is a luxury you cannot afford. It is no coincidence that high levels of poverty and unemployment are endemic in areas where there is a high concentration of endangered wildlife species.

BARBARY MACAQUE

Macaca sylvanus
Endangered

The Barbary macaque is the only surviving primate in Africa north of the Sahara. Historically distributed across parts of Europe and all of northern Africa, it is now limited to small remaining patches of forest and scrub in Algeria and Morocco. The population is estimated to have declined by over 50% in the last quarter century, and this is expected to continue. Its main threat is habitat loss due to intensive logging, charcoal burning, firewood collecting, and land clearance for agriculture. Further habitat degradation resulting from overgrazing by livestock, exacerbated by drought, is expected to affect the long-term future of the species.

◄   *Despite their large canines, Barbary macaques are largely herbivorous.*

▶▶ *Overleaf: Unlike other macaques, males participate in rearing the young, including time spent playing and grooming. Confronted by multiple threats, the Barbary macaque faces a doubtful future.*

MOUNTAIN GORILLA

Gorilla beringei ssp. *beringei*
Endangered

Mountain gorillas live in the
Virunga Mountains of Rwanda,
Uganda and Democratic
Republic of Congo, an area
of fast-growing human
population density. Habitat
destruction and exploitation of
forest resources are escalating,
and poaching, particularly for
bushmeat, is on the increase.
Continued civil and political
volatility, in particular the
deadly war in Congo, mean the
gorillas are acutely vulnerable.
Tourism is a key conservation
strategy, despite concerns
about disease transmission
and disturbance. Protected by
guards and daily monitoring,
gorillas visited by tourists have
consistently fared better than
non-habituated groups.

▶   *Surrounding cultivation
    confines the gorillas of
    the Virunga Mountains
    to altitudes above
    1,500 m (5,000 ft).*

▶▶ *Overleaf: Young
    gorillas at play.*

▶▶ *Following pages, left: The
    resurgence of poaching
    is one of many threats
    to mountain gorillas.*

▶▶ *Following pages, right:
    A mother cradles her
    ten-day-old baby.*

ON THE FRONTLINE:
RWANDA

The mountain gorillas of Rwanda are a rare success story in recent conservation history. Here is proof that with the right attitude, the will to succeed, and the power to act, it is possible to pull a species back from the brink of disaster. After years of poaching, persecution and destruction of their habitat, the gorillas are on the verge of extinction. Nonetheless, a 2004 census of gorilla populations showed an increase of 17% since 1989, despite Rwanda suffering in 1994 one of the swiftest, most brutal genocides in human history.

The key to Rwanda's conservation success is community-based eco-tourism. The government, with the help of outside non-governmental organizations (predominantly the Mountain Gorilla Project), has developed an entire industry around its population of gorillas. This is well organized, well managed and profitable: annual revenues in excess of US$7 million make it the country's third-highest foreign currency generator after tea and coffee (source: Rwandan Office of Tourism and National Parks, or ORTPN). Importantly, the tourism industry directly benefits the local villagers,

those people living on the edge of the forests that the gorillas inhabit. In the past, the villagers would use the forest to harvest timber for building and firewood, as well as for hunting animals such as deer for food. Directly and indirectly, such activities impacted on the gorillas, which were often caught inadvertently in traps and snares, or were killed in confrontations with human trespassers who accidentally crossed their paths.

In total around 76% of the jobs related to gorilla tourism are filled by local villagers, which ensures that those people affected most by the presence of the national park, with all its associated rules and restrictions, benefit the most from the tourist dollar the park generates. And there are additional benefits. As well as the jobs directly related to tourism – forest rangers, trackers, guards, porters, guides – the government set up a scheme of revenue-sharing that diverts 5% of income generated through gorilla tourism directly to the villagers. The money they receive pays for wood and food, negating the need to plunder these vital resources from within the national park boundaries, and thus reducing the potential

▶ *Carefully managed gorilla tourism is central to conservation efforts in Rwanda.*

for human/gorilla conflict. To the same end, an 80-km (50-mile) dry-stone wall has been built along the park boundary to keep grazing animals inside. This protects crops grown by farmers owning land abutting the park. No longer concerned with the potential loss of their crops, the farmers have ceased laying snares to catch deer and, as a result, accidental mortality of gorillas has been all but eradicated.

Local communities also benefit indirectly from the tourism programme. Road building to aid tourism has had the knock-on effect of making it easier and cheaper for farmers to transport their products to market. The national treasury has also provided funding for community-based projects. For example, in 2008 ORTPN unveiled community facilities including a community lodge, health centres, school classrooms and water tanks costing Frw410 million (US$750,000) in Musanze and Bulera, two districts along the frontier of the national park.

While recognizing that there is still much to be done to secure the gorillas' future, the steps taken by the Rwandan authorities are clearly working for both the community and for the animals. The villages around the national park are thriving and the wounds from the events of 1994 are healing. Rwanda's gorillas are also thriving. Each year the park authorities hold a 'Kwita Izina' – a naming ceremony. This is advertised countrywide and is an opportunity for all Rwandans

◄ *A baby mountain gorilla in Rwanda, where the population is growing thanks to a scheme that rewards local communities and ensures that they benefit directly from the financial windfall of tourism.*

to become involved in the naming of young gorillas. Between 2005, when the first ceremony took place, and 2007, 80 gorillas were given names. A further 20 gorillas were named in 2008, when festivities lasted a week and included concerts, community work, a national conference and the unveiling of a gorilla monument in an effort to highlight the progress made in promoting government/community partnerships in gorilla conservation.

As Theodore Mgerageze, a porter in one of the villages that skirt the edge of the forest, told me: 'Before tourism gorillas had no meaning to us because we got no benefit from their being here. Now the whole village looks out for the gorillas, protects them, because we earn our living from the tourism they bring.'

WESTERN LOWLAND GORILLA

Gorilla gorilla ssp. *gorilla*
Critically endangered

Western lowland gorillas had until recently an almost continuous distribution from the Central African Republic to the coast. But in the last three generations their numbers have dropped by more than 80%. Unlike their mountain cousins, habitat loss is not a major cause of ape decline in this region. Indeed, much of their traditional forest habitat remains intact. Instead, commercial hunting and outbreaks of the Ebola virus are to blame. National and international laws controlling hunting are in place in all relevant countries, but enforcement is almost non-existent. Urgent conservation efforts are needed if the species is to survive.

◄ *Western lowland gorilla groups are typically comprised of between 10 and 20 individuals, with one dominant adult male.*

◄◄ *Staple foods are pith, leaves and shoots.*

CHIMPANZEE

Pan troglodytes
Endangered

Although chimpanzees are the most abundant of the apes, with a wide though non-continuous distribution in Equatorial Africa, populations have declined significantly due to poaching (particularly for bushmeat); habitat loss and degradation; and disease, including Ebola and human-transmitted diseases. Chimpanzees are legally protected in most countries. However, conservation of the species urgently requires stricter law enforcement and better management of protected areas. Engagement with commercial hunters serving central Africa's bushmeat trade is essential. Economic alternatives to hunting and land-extensive agriculture must be supported.

▶ *The chimpanzee's main predator is the leopard, and groups must remain alert at all times.*

▶▶ *Chimpanzees are both arboreal and terrestrial, spending equal time in the trees and on the ground.*

▶▶ *Overleaf: Chimpanzees share a high percentage of DNA with humans, making them our closest living relative.*

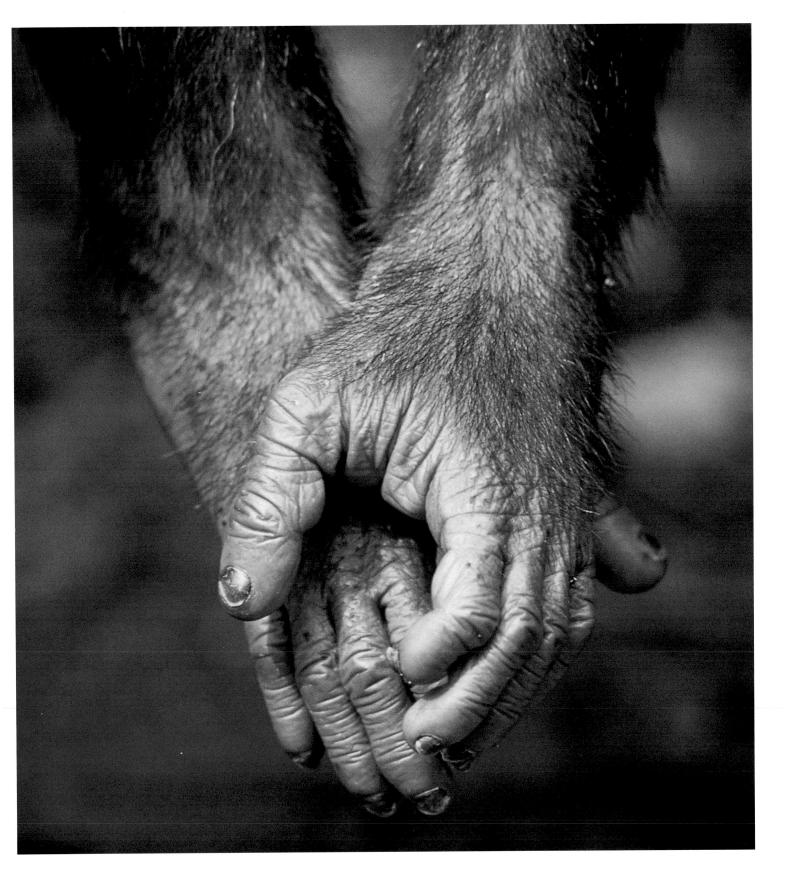

BONOBO

Pan paniscus
Endangered

Bonobos inhabit a discontinuous range in the low-lying central Congo Basin, south of the Congo River. This is a region of rapidly increasing human population density and a high degree of political instability. Poaching is the species' principal threat, driven by commercialization of the bushmeat trade. Although bonobos are legally protected, law enforcement is negligible. Hunters, aided by military and local administration, are active in all areas, including supposedly protected areas such as Salonga National Park. NGOs are using participatory approaches to guide local communities towards the sustainable use of natural resources for long-term conservation.

▶ *The formation of the Congo River likely led to the separate evolution of the bonobo, which, together with the common chimpanzee, constitutes the genus Pan.*

▶▶ *Overleaf, left: Bonobos' forelimb 'palm walking' is in contrast to chimpanzees' predominant use of knuckles.*

▶▶ *Overleaf, right: The strong mother–son bond often continues throughout life.*

ON THE FRONTLINE:
CONGO

At the heart of the African continent, at the meeting point between three central African nations, lie Dzanga-Sangha Special Reserve (Central African Republic), Nouabale Ndoki National Park (Democratic Republic of Congo) and Lobeke National Park (Cameroon). Together these form the Sangha River Tri-national Conservation Area, created on the initiative of the Central Africa Forests Commission to coordinate police efforts against poaching, trade in illegal goods such as ivory and arms, and illegal fishing and hunting.

In September 2007 I travelled to two of the parks, Dzanga-Sangha and Nouabale Ndoki, in order to photograph wild lowland gorillas and to assess the effects of the logging trade on the wildlife of the region.

Forests cover nearly two-thirds of Congo, providing work for 10% of the population. Timber products account for around 7% of the country's gross national product – it's second largest export after oil – and production has more than doubled in the past decade. In short, the forest is a vital resource in the economic welfare of the nation.

This is even more the case in the Central African Republic, where timber accounts for around 16% of

exports, second only to diamonds, and the forestry sector is a bigger employer than any other private industry. Over 3,500 people work in the timber trade, and those 3,500 support many more – family members who are too old, too young or too ill to work. This is despite the fact that their average income is the equivalent of just US$1.25 for an eight-hour day.

With few alternatives, logging is for many people the only way they are able to earn a living. But these forests also support a wealth of wildlife, including endangered species such as western lowland gorillas, chimpanzees and forest elephants, as well as providing a natural protection against global warming. This inevitably generates conflict between conservationists and local people.

In the Central African Republic I spoke to Ngapé Anicet, former Assistant Personnel Director at the Societé de Bois de Bayanga timber company. He told me that the plant had been closed down and all 450 staff laid off, though business was thriving. The workers were given no reason for the closure but its suddenness implied political intervention. Unconfirmed rumours around Bayanga

► Poaching of elephants for ivory and meat has increased in one area of Congo where a logging plant supporting thousands of villagers was closed due to political pressure.

village claimed the local authorities had come under pressure from one of the global conservation charities.

On a wooden veranda, sharing an ice-cold coke, Ngapé explained to me his village's history.

'Before the plant opened we used to fish and grow crops. There was no real future for our children, simply survival. Then the plant opened and created new and diverse jobs. All of a sudden we needed engineers, carpenters and accountants. The timber company brought us hope. It gave our kids jobs to aspire to. Then it was gone. We employed 450 people, each one in turn supporting an average of ten family members on their salary from the plant. Now those people have no income, no jobs – they are desperate.'

He compared the closing of the plant without any thought to how the workers would support themselves with the disaster of invading Iraq without a plan for what would follow the military victory. 'In both cases', he told me, 'you get chaos.'

I asked him what the former workers were doing now.

'Some have left their homes and their family and headed to the city to look for work,' he replied. 'But many more have reverted to illegal logging and poaching wildlife. They can get up to twenty times what the plant paid them per month for an elephant. Before, when they had a job and a future, they weren't interested in poaching. Now, they do what they must to survive.'

I asked him whether the village had received any help.

'The village has been given some money from philanthropists and from charities but the money is mismanaged and it isn't reaching the people it is intended for. If people really want to help then the answer is to come here and give to the people directly.'

I countered that deforestation is not only adding to global warming, it is placing in greater peril some of the region's most iconic wildlife species. 'I am a

conservationist,' Ngapé responded. 'I agree that we should protect the forest. But why can't logging be sustainable? Sustainable logging is practised elsewhere under the guidance of ECOFAC [the African Conservation Foundation]. Why can't we do the same here?'

Ngapé was fearful of what the future held in store for Bayanga village. But he had some suggestions for setting up micro-economic agricultural projects (his words, not mine), including poultry farming, pig farming and cottage gardening. 'All we need', he pleaded, 'is a little help to set these programmes up.'

Like most of the people I interviewed, Ngapé is not asking for the earth. He isn't seeking a million-dollar grant or even state welfare payments. He doesn't expect handouts, much less sympathy. He just wants to be able to feed his family and enjoy the odd bottle of local beer. He wants life to be a little bit easier. Don't we ask for the same?

◄ *Commercial trade in bushmeat is the predominat threat to lowland gorillas in central Africa.*

PAINTED HUNTING DOG

Lycaon pictus
Endangered

Painted hunting dogs once ranged across much of sub-Saharan Africa. Today they total around just 3,500–5,000, and are found only in southern and eastern Africa. Their numbers continue to decline due to ongoing conflict with humans, disease and habitat fragmentation. Although legally protected across much of their range, this is rarely enforced. Outside reserves, legal protection may serve only to alienate remote communities that come into conflict with hunting dogs and whose cooperation may well be essential to the future of the species. Conservation priorities include maintaining suitable habitat and creating links between habitat regions.

▶ *Hunting dogs pursue their prey in a long, open chase that may cover several kilometres. Nearly 80% of all hunts end in a kill.*

▶▶ *Overleaf: They are generalist predators whose preferred habitats include short-grass plains, semi-desert, bushy savannas and upland forest. The dogs rest after a hunt.*

BLACK RHINOCEROS

Diceros bicornis
Critically endangered

The main threat to the black rhinoceros is poaching for its horn. Feared extinct in its former territories in central-west Africa, it is now found only in east and southern Africa. War, civil unrest, poverty and the free flow of weapons have significantly impacted conservation efforts in recent decades. Lack of political will and authority have led to diminished protection, increases in poaching and the trading of horns for weapons. However, there has been an increase in numbers in recent years thanks to efforts to concentrate remaining rhinos in fenced conservation areas.

◄　*The black rhino has a reputation for aggression, but attacks are usually driven by fear, confusion or panic.*

►►　*Overleaf: Horns are used for defense, intimidation, digging up roots and breaking branches. Terrible eyesight is compensated by large ears that rotate to detect sound, and an excellent sense of smell.*

►►　*Following pages: Black rhinoceroses avoid open grassland, frequented by the white rhinoceros, preferring the edges of wooded areas.*

GREVY'S ZEBRA

Equus grevyi
Endangered

Estimates put the total population of Grevy's zebra at between 2,000 and 2,500 individuals, a decline of over 50% in two decades. This is attributed to reduced availability of water, habitat degradation and loss through overgrazing, competition for resources, and hunting. In Kenya, the decline is linked to diminished reproduction rates due to high juvenile mortality, a consequence of competition for resources with pastoral people and their livestock. In Ethiopia, hunting is the primary cause of decline. Recently both Kenya and Ethiopia have taken steps towards conservation. And in areas where community-based conservation is promoted and ongoing, there are signs of success.

◄ *Males fight over territory and females, vocalizing loudly as they duel.*

◄◄ *Close-set stripes that extend to the hooves distinguish the Grevy's zebra from the more common Burchell's zebra.*

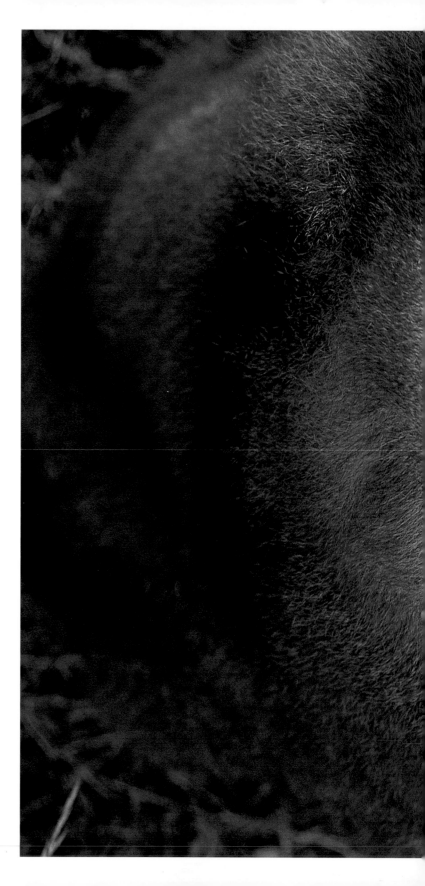

DRILL

Mandrillus leucophaeus
Endangered

Drills occupy a small range in southwest Cameroon and southeast Nigeria, and are severely threatened by habitat loss. They have been totally displaced in the heart of their range by clear-felling and human settlement. Although some reforestation has occurred, mostly it has involved the planting of inedible exotic species such as eucalyptus. The drill is also hunted for the bushmeat trade. Roads built to facilitate logging also open up forest areas for cultivators, leading to further habitat loss, as well as enabling commercial hunters to penetrate ever more deeply into the forests. Farmers also frequently kill drills to protect their crops, and such incidents are likely to increase as cultivation expands.

◄ *Drills are uncommon in all parts of their range but they have managed to persist in a number of areas where they were presumed to be extinct.*

GOLDEN-CROWNED SIFAKA

Propithecus tattersalli
Endangered

This species has a restricted distribution in northeastern Madagascar. The forests throughout its range have been reduced to remnant tracts separated by degraded grasslands. Hunting by migrant gold miners is considered the largest current and future threat, although slash-and-burn agriculture, uncontrolled grass fires, wood extraction for housing and firewood, logging of precious hardwoods, and gold mining in general also pose significant threats. A new protected area was established in the Daraina region in 2005. This 20,000 hectare (50,000 acre) zone is managed by a local NGO, Association Fanamby, in collaboration with the Ministry of Water and Forests.

▶ *The golden-crowned sifaka has a restricted distribution, limited to forest patches in northeastern Madagascar. Sifakas are lemurs, and are found only on the island of Madagascar.*

CROWNED SIFAKA

Propithecus coronatus
Endangered

The crowned sifaka inhabits an area of western Madagascar. The main threat to the species is habitat loss. Forests within its range have been destroyed to provide pasture for livestock and to produce charcoal. Hunting, predominantly for the pet trade, is also thought to occur in some areas. The population is believed to have undergone a reduction of more than 50% over the past 30 years. Conservation efforts to secure protection for populations throughout the range are needed if the species is to survive.

◀ *Crowned sifakas primarily inhabit dry deciduous forests, although they are sometimes found in mangroves.*

BLACK-AND-WHITE RUFFED LEMUR

Varecia variegata
Critically endangered

The black-and-white ruffed lemur is very patchily distributed in lowland to mid-altitude rainforests in eastern Madagascar. The principal threat to its survival is habitat loss due to slash-and-burn agriculture, logging and mining. It is also among the most heavily hunted of all lemur species. It has a loud, raucous call, and increased levels of hunting have been linked to the seasonality of its vocalizations, which increase with food availability. In Makira, in northeastern Madagascar, this species is one of the more expensive and desired meats, and hunting is largely unsustainable. This is one of the first lemurs to disappear when humans encroach upon rainforest habitats.

▶ *Black-and-white ruffed lemurs are very selective feeders, surviving almost exclusively on fruit. This makes them especially susceptible to disturbance.*

RED RUFFED LEMUR

Varecia rubra
Endangered

The red ruffed lemur has a restricted range in northeastern Madagascar, chiefly inhabiting the remaining primary forests of the Masoala Peninsula and the region immediately north of the Bay of Antongil. The species is threatened by human encroachment and habitat loss, particularly due to slash-and-burn agriculture. Hunting also remains a threat. It is officially protected only within the Masoala National Park and the Makira Protected Area, and increased regulation and management of hunting is needed if conservation efforts are to be successful.

◄ *It is believed that red ruffed lemurs have a vocabulary of 12 different calls.*

DIADEMED SIFAKA

Propithecus diadema
Endangered

The diademed sifaka occurs in very low densities throughout the eastern rainforests of Madagascar. Continued destruction of rainforest habitat in its range, due to slash-and-burn agriculture and timber extraction, is the principal threat to the species' survival, although hunting for food is also having a very serious impact on remaining populations, even within existing protected areas. The planting of sugar cane fields for the illegal production of rum is also a threat in certain parts of its range.

▶ *The diademed sifaka is a prosimian, a type of primate that has evolved independently of other primates for about 55 million years.*

▶▶ *Long white fur encircling the muzzle and covering cheeks, forehead and chin creates the appearance of a diadem or crown.*

INDRI

Indri indri
Endangered

The indri is a lemur related to
the sifaka, and like all lemurs
is native to Madagascar. It
inhabits the island's eastern
tropical moist-lowland and
montane forests. The species
is threatened by habitat loss as
forests are cut down to supply
fuel and timber and for slash-
and-burn agriculture. Many
local people consider hunting
of the indri to be taboo, but
that tradition has broken down
in some regions and hunting
is now a significant problem,
with current levels considered
unsustainable. Conservation
efforts are under way,
including a proposal to create
a protected area of the corridor
between Mantadia and
Zahamena. A major region-
wide conservation education
campaign is required to
discourage hunting, with the
indri as the flagship species.

▶ *Indris have perhaps the
loudest high-pitched call
of any terrestrial animal.
Their distinctive 'song' can
last over three minutes.*

▶▶ *Population densities are
low: indris live in groups
of 2–6 individuals, usually
a monogamous pair with
their offspring. Their
numbers are declining.*

AYE-AYE

Daubentonia
madagascariensis
Near threatened

Once believed to be very
rare and primarily a denizen
of Madagascar's eastern
rainforest, since the 1980s
the aye-aye has been found in
many new localities. Current
opinion is that the species may
be the most widely distributed
of Madagascar's lemurs.
Consquently its status was
changed from Endangered
(2000) to Near Threatened
(2008). But nonetheless it is
believed to have undergone
a 20–25% decline in the past
quarter century, and nowhere
is it in abundance. It is still
regarded as a harbinger of
evil and killed as a pest, and
habitat destruction remains a
localized threat throughout its
range. In addition, trees that
are among its dietary staples
are cut preferentially for the
construction of boats, houses
and coffins.

▶   *The nocturnal aye-aye*
    is quite adaptable,
    and is found in a wide
    range of habitats across
    Madagascar. It uses its
    elongated middle finger
    to pull grubs out of trees.

PYGMY HIPPOPOTAMUS

Choeropsis liberiensis
Endangered

The pygmy hippopotamus is rarely seen because of its secretive, nocturnal habits. It is endemic to western Africa, with known populations in Liberia, Côte d'Ivoire, Guinea and Sierra Leone. In 1993 the species was estimated at 2,000–3,000 individuals. Current numbers are not known, but forests within its historic range have been steadily logged, farmed and settled in recent years, and human development has caused its retreat into diminishing, fragmented parcels of forest. Opportunistic kills by bushmeat hunters do occur, although it is not typically a primary target for subsistence hunting. The pygmy hippopotamus has also been impacted by war in its native territories. It is legally protected in all countries, but enforcement is poor.

▶ *Largely nocturnal, pygmy hippopotamuses tend to spend the day hidden in swamps, wallows or rivers, and sometimes in hollows under the banks of streams.*

EAST, WEST & SOUTH ASIA

This chapter surveys an extensive area from the Middle East, through the former Soviet Bloc countries of Central Asia, to China, Korea and Japan, as well as the Indian subcontinent. This ecologically and geographically diverse zone hosts nearly a fifth of the world's most endangered mammals, including global icons of the natural world such as the tiger, snow leopard, giant panda and Asian elephant.

The habitats across the region are numerous and varied, from the sands of the Middle East to the mountains of the Himalayas, the vast plateaus of China, and north to the immense Gobi Desert, the fourth largest in the world, straddling northern China and southern Mongolia. However, once again, it is the great forests that sustain the majority of endangered mammals (62%), though a significant minority are reliant on grasslands, shrublands, savannahs and deserts.

Nearly two-thirds of all endangered species in these areas of the world are threatened by the development of land for agriculture and by harvesting of biological resources. This is no surprise given that the human populations of China and India together account for over a third of the world's total. And, as both country's populations continue to grow, and more and more land is claimed for agriculture, building and development, human encroachment remains a grave threat.

Pollution is another noteworthy concern. China's rise as an economic power, as well as that of India, has been unparalleled, but so too is the consequent pollution problem. Environmental degradation is now so severe that this poses a major risk to people as well as wildlife. Only 1% of China's 560 million city dwellers breathe air that is considered safe by European Union standards, and nearly 40% of the population have no access to safe drinking water. Pollution is also a major concern in India, with the World Bank estimating that by 2020 the country's water, air, soil and forest resources will be under more pressure from humans than those of any other country.

China and India are also failing to stop the illegal trade in wildlife, which continues to undermine efforts to save some of the region's most iconic species. India is the source for the majority of poached tigers whose body parts end up in China, where they are in great demand for use in traditional medicine. China is also the final destination and hub for the trade in snow leopard pelts. Soaring earning power, driven by China's huge economic success of recent years, has led to much greater individual wealth and many Chinese are now able to afford and feel they have earned such 'luxuries'.

I spoke to one Chinese family who had recently bought a tiger pelt to adorn their living room floor. When I politely suggested that the family's purchase was of questionable ethics, the head of the family retorted: 'Your kings once roamed India and Africa shooting anything in sight to nail a trophy to their palace walls. What is good enough for your kings is good enough for us.'

It is a hard argument to counter. Looking back on the past of the countries of Europe and the United States, it is debatable whether our ancestors behaved any better when they reaped the rewards of colonialism and an industrial revolution that is now being repeated in parts of Asia. Until all developed countries learn the lessons of the past, and commit to supporting countries in the developing world to preserve their natural heritage while also expanding their economies, it is hard to feel optimistic of the chances of real change.

SNOW LEOPARD

Panthera uncia
Endangered

The snow leopard is restricted to the high mountains of Central Asia. Populations have declined by 20% in less than two decades. Strong demand in China for pelts as well as body parts for traditional medicine has led to severe and ongoing losses to poaching. Over-stocking of high-altitude grasslands with livestock is widespread, leading to decline in the wild prey base and an increase in retributive killing when leopards raid livestock. Conservation priorities include promoting practices that reduce livestock vulnerability, and providing financial incentives to communities to conserve the species, including wildlife-based eco-tourism and the development of alternative sources of income, for example handicrafts.

▶ *Snow leopards generally live at elevations of 3,000– 4,500 m (10,000–15,000 ft).*

▶▶ *Overleaf: Cold, arid conditions mean their natural prey – wild sheep and ibex – are inherently sparse.*

▶▶ *Following pages: The snow leopard favours steep terrain broken by cliffs, ridges and rocky outcrops. Its markings provide excellent camouflage.*

MARKHOR

Capra falconeri
Endangered

The markhor is a large wild goat found in woodland areas of the Western Himalayas. Habitat loss is a contributor to declining populations, but the primary threat to markhor numbers throughout the range is hunting, both for its meat and also its horns, used in traditional medicines. Poaching controls in Pakistan's Chitral Gol National Park have been successful, and other populations would benefit from similar protection. Alternatively, programmes such as the Torghar Conservation Project in Baluchistan may prove a successful conservation model, with carefully managed, sustainable trophy hunting used to raise funds for the local community.

▶ *Their high value as a trophy species means markhor are sought after by hunters.*

▶▶ *Markhor are adapted to mountainous terrain. They are most active in the early morning and late afternoon.*

WILD BACTRIAN CAMEL

Camelus ferus
Critically endangered

The Bactrian camel inhabits the deserts of China and Mongolia. By 2004, there were approximately 600 individuals in China and 350 in Mongolia, with numbers continuing to decrease. Part of its range in China was used for 45 years as a nuclear test site, but the species survived and is apparently breeding naturally. However, it now faces new threats including highly toxic illegal mining and impending industrial encroachment (gas pipeline laying, exploitation of minerals). Subsistence hunting for food and hybridization are also major threats. A recently established captive breeding programme is seen as an urgent conservation priority. With only 15 individuals in captivity, the whole species could be wiped out if its natural habitat is destroyed.

◄　By the mid-19th century, Bactrian camels had been extirpated from the western part of their range and persisted only in remote areas of the Gobi and Taklimakan deserts.

▶▶　Overleaf: The camels' desert habitat varies from rocky mountain massifs to flat, arid areas. Vegetation is sparse.

GIANT PANDA

Ailuropoda melanoleuca
Endangered

The giant panda is confined to south-central China. Restricted, degraded habitat is the species' greatest threat. Logging and land clearance for farming have resulted in small, isolated populations across six mountain ranges, confined to high ridges and hemmed in by cultivation. Within these areas, bamboo forest is separated by patches of cleared land and forest without a bamboo understorey. The Chinese authorities have established a network of reserves and linkages between some of these patches of habitat, but population size and limited range still threaten the survival of the species.

▶ *Bamboo comprises 99% of the giant panda's diet, making it especially vulnerable to habitat degradation.*

RED PANDA

Ailurus fulgens
Vulnerable

The distribution of red pandas in the wild is poorly known, but includes Nepal, India, Bhutan, Myanmar and southern China. Principal threats to the species are loss and fragmentation of habitat and poaching. The human population within its range and in surrounding areas almost doubled between 1971 and 1991, creating increased pressure on land for both housing and farming, as well as increased demand for firewood. Conservation recommendations include expansion and strengthening of the protected area network, prevention of illegal felling, control of grazing and slash-and-burn shifting cultivation, regulation of tourism, public education campaigns and enforcement of existing legal protection. Its classification was downgraded from Endangered to Vulnerable in 2008.

◀ *In parts of China, the red panda and giant panda inhabit the same terrain.*

▶▶ *Overleaf: Red pandas are largely arboreal. They are shy and secretive in nature, with mostly nocturnal habits.*

UPLAND BARASINGHA

Rucervus duvaucelii branderi
Endangered

The barasingha is a species of deer native to India and Nepal. Its present distribution is much reduced and fragmented by habitat loss and barely restrained hunting. A population of 300–350 of the subspecies *branderi* survives only in Kanha National Park in Madhya Pradesh. However, habitat degradation is ongoing even within the park due to timber and fuel-wood cutting by local people, while poaching for antlers and meat also continues. Conservation activities have included dispersal of tigers away from main grazing areas, implementation of poaching controls, cessation of grass burning, creation of water reservoirs and a reduction in domestic cattle. Out-migration of villages from the park has significantly extended barasingha habitat, protecting their traditional fawning and rutting grounds.

▶ *Barasingha disperse in the wet season and congregate in large herds during the dry season, often in response to new growth following fire and the need for drinking water.*

RED SLENDER LORIS

Loris tardigradus
Endangered

The red slender loris is a small primate endemic to central and southwestern Sri Lanka and is typically found in the forests of the island's southern wet zone. The threats it faces include habitat loss to agriculture, road accidents, hunting for the illegal pet trade and traditional medicine and superstitious killing. Recent population studies estimate low numbers in fragmented forest patches. It appears to require continuous canopy in order to move between forest patches, and it is evident that both subspecies *L.t.nycticeboides* and *L.t.tardigradus* are in decline.

◄   *The red slender loris exists in a few isolated forest patches that are undergoing severe encroachment by humans.*

LION-TAILED MACAQUE

Macaca silenus
Endangered

Lion-tailed macaques are endemic to the Western Ghats hill ranges of southwestern India. They are mainly arboreal, preferring the upper canopy of primary tropical evergreen rainforest. Habitat fragmentation and loss, due mainly to timber harvesting and clearance for exotic plantations such as tea, eucalyptus and coffee, are the species' main threats. In one location, Coorg, where there remains a large area of wet evergreen habitat, the species is threatened by commercial and subsistence hunting for food. Management of private lands, which hold perhaps a quarter of the remaining population, is needed: this would ideally include maintaining coffee and cardamom plantations where populations remain (the species cannot persist on tea plantations).

◀ *The total wild population of lion-tailed macaques is estimated to be less than 4,000, made up of small, isolated sub-populations.*

◀◀ *Hunting to supply the local pet trade is one of a range of threats facing this species.*

GREATER ONE-HORNED RHINOCEROS

Rhinoceros unicornis
Vulnerable

Greater one-horned rhinoceros numbers are increasing overall thanks to strict protection, particularly in India. As a result the species was reclassified from Endangered to Vulnerable in 2008. However, some sub-populations are still in decline, especially those in Nepal, which have suffered due to political instability. The species is confined to fewer than ten sites and is severely fragmented. Deterioration in habitat quality is projected to continue; if not halted, this will affect the long-term survival of some smaller populations, and could jeopardize the further recovery of the species.

◀ *Active mostly at night and in the early morning, during the day rhinoceroses wallow in water to keep cool.*

◀◀ *The greater one-horned rhino prefers tall grasslands and riverine forests, but habitat loss has forced it onto more cultivated land.*

▶▶ *Overleaf: Mothers will stay close to their calves for up to four years after birth.*

▶▶ *Following pages: Rhinoceroses are grazers, using a continuous rocking motion to tear up grass.*

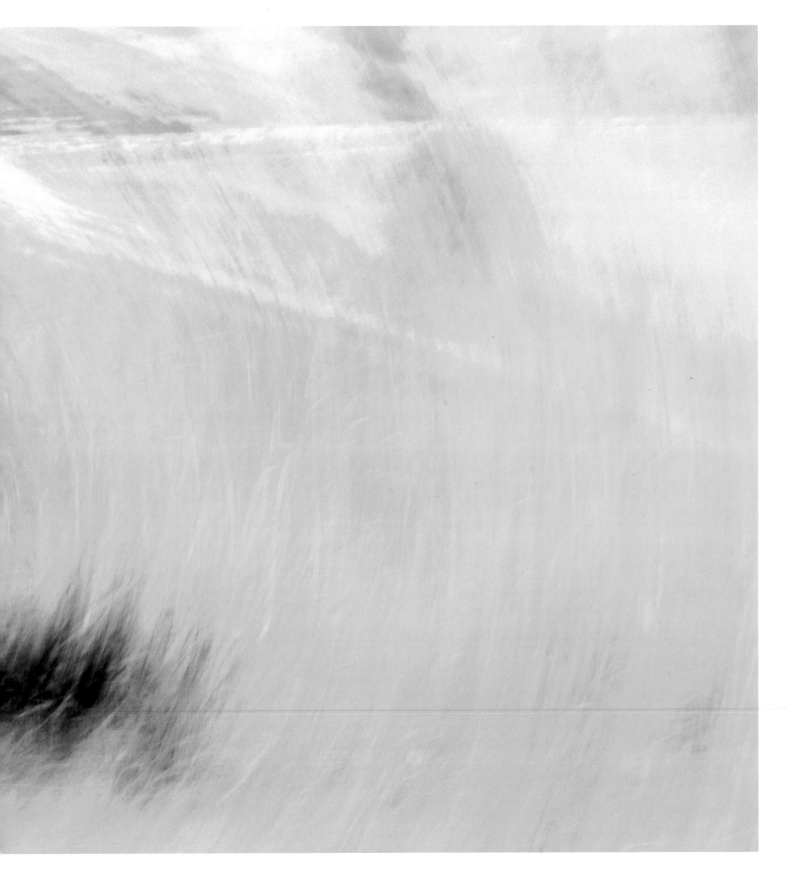

ON THE FRONTLINE:
NEPAL

There is a sense of foreboding on entering a prison, particularly at the moment that the door to the outside world is banged shut and locked behind you. All of a sudden, even the most banal life can seem very appealing. Of course, I was fortunate. My visit was both voluntary and temporary. I was in Nepal to talk to wildlife poachers, to try to understand their motives.

My interviewee, let's call him Fanishwar, was led from a small, dark cell that he shared with two other people. He looked tired and much older than his actual age. He is 28 and was caught poaching rhinos in Chitwan National Park. He will be over 45 by the time he gets out of prison, assuming he doesn't die first. I don't expect you to feel sorry for him, or any of the other poachers languishing in jails in Nepal, India and elsewhere. Most of them were well aware of the risks they took and must accept the consequences. I know many people who would feel that justice will have been served only if Fanishwar never sees freedom again. But that is to see just one side of the story. Because Fanishwar isn't the problem, and focusing on him gets us no closer to resolving the real issue.

Fanishwar sits across a small table from me on a wooden chair. The room we share is featureless and grey, like Fanishwar's life. I asked him straight out, why had he killed rhinos? He didn't answer, just looked down at the table, avoiding eye contact. So I tried a different tack and asked him about his life.

Like many people in Nepal, Fanishwar lived in poverty. And I don't mean poverty as we define it in the West. I mean the sort of poverty where the first thing you do on waking in the morning is check to see which of your children are still alive. On the day Fanishwar's life changed, his youngest, a boy aged 18 months, wasn't.

That day, Fanishwar reacted as I suspect any parent would. He felt compelled to do anything necessary to protect his remaining family. He knew of a man in the local area. This man had an air of wealth, of success. He had a way with words, and he was well-connected at a high level. He was also known to have helped improve the standard of living of other impoverished people – people like Fanishwar. Maybe he could help him too.

The man spun for Fanishwar a colourful story: there were plenty of rhinos left in the wild, the stories he had heard to the contrary were just propaganda. There was no chance that Fanishwar would get caught and, if he did, then the man would be there to help him. He would be safe. His family would be safe. And, most alluring of all, Fanishwar would be paid the equivalent of US$200 for a single rhino horn – almost a year's salary. Fanishwar started dreaming of a better life for his family. A life where he could provide regular food, a warm, dry home, possibly even buy a bicycle.

This is how it happens. This is how regular, law-abiding folk like Fanishwar end up as poachers. And for every Fanishwar that we put in jail there are hundreds more to fill his shoes. There is no shortage of people living in abject poverty in Nepal, nor in India, China, Indonesia, Malaysia, the Philippines ... the list goes on.

Patrick Brown is an Australian-born photographer based in Southeast Asia. There, among other things, he has worked on a project documenting the illegal trade in wildlife. In a recent interview he observed that 'only the ignorant and often desperate poachers get caught.' Referring to his experiences, Brown went on to say: 'I actually feel sorry for the poachers. I empathize with them quite a lot – not with what they are doing but with the situation that they are in. For example, these guys are going to get at the most US$250 for a rhino horn. A rhino horn in weight is five times more valuable than gold by the time it gets to Hong Kong or the Middle East, or even to the States or Europe. They are fuelling the market, but the poacher is being fuelled by other needs – the need to keep a family alive, poverty, etc.

'Then you have your middleman or trader at the forefront of the stockpiles, the harvesting grounds. This is the man I dislike most of all. He's the one that encourages, entices, tells the poachers and their families that there's nothing to be risked. These are the smooth-talking guys; the guys that you can't get to. They know the risks. They know that if they get photographed or met by a foreigner then their whole cover is blown. They're the nasty guys and no mud sticks to them, they never get caught.

'This guy also is in cahoots, usually, with local governments, either on a council level or right up to the state government. Otherwise he would not be able to survive.

'On a par with him are the government officials. They know what's happening but they turn a blind eye, because their wallets – or their uncle's or whoever's wallet – are getting filled and they let things happen.

'The salesman in the markets, in Hong Kong, China or Japan, or wherever, he's just selling a product to demand, it could be mobile phones, he doesn't really care to be honest.'

At the end of my interview with Fanishwar I asked him again, why had he killed the rhinos? This time he didn't lower his head. He looked at me for a long minute, his eyes moist. Then he simply said, 'Because I love my children.'

Fanishwar is no longer a threat to wildlife. He's in prison and will be there for a long time to come. But does that make the rhinos of Nepal any safer from extinction? I suspect not. So here's an idea. What if we found a way of helping the next Fanishwar buy a bicycle, a means of earning a living less dangerous than killing rhinos? What if we did that? Perhaps then, when the well-connected, smooth-talking man turned up in his neighbourhood, he would be too busy working to give him the time of day.

ASIAN ELEPHANT

Elephas maximus
Endangered

Even within its remaining range in South and Southeast Asia, the Asian elephant has been in decline for centuries, and survives only in highly fragmented populations. This is the area of the world with the densest human population. As human populations increase and encroach upon elephant habitat, so too does human/elephant conflict increase when elephants eat or trample crops. Poaching for ivory also remains a major threat. Conservation priorities include maintaining habitat zones and corridors, as well as managing human/elephant conflict as part of an integrated land-use policy that recognizes elephants as economic assets from which local people may benefit, or at least not suffer.

▶ *Elephant herds follow well-defined seasonal migration routes. Farms established on these routes can suffer substantial crop damage.*

▶▶ *Overleaf: Elephants need to drink 80–200 litres (20–50 gallons) of water a day, and use more for bathing.*

▶▶ *Following pages: Elephant charges are often displays of aggression that go no further than threats.*

TIGER

Panthera tigris
Endangered

The tiger once ranged widely across Asia but conversion of forest areas to agriculture, commercial logging and human settlement has resulted in a 93% decrease in its historic range. Where suitable habitat does exist, prey base depletion is a major threat, and persistent poaching of tigers for Asian medicine is driving the species to extinction. There have been numerous conservation efforts in recent years but the most effective measures, according to a recent study, are education of local people, especially children, and better training, provision and financial support for protected area staff.

◄　*Tigers usually hunt at night, alone.*

◄◄　*Tigers need to kill 50 large prey animals a year. Attacks on livestock and people can lead to significant conflict with local communities.*

►►　*Overleaf: Tigers are generally solitary, with adults maintaining exclusive territories, or home ranges.*

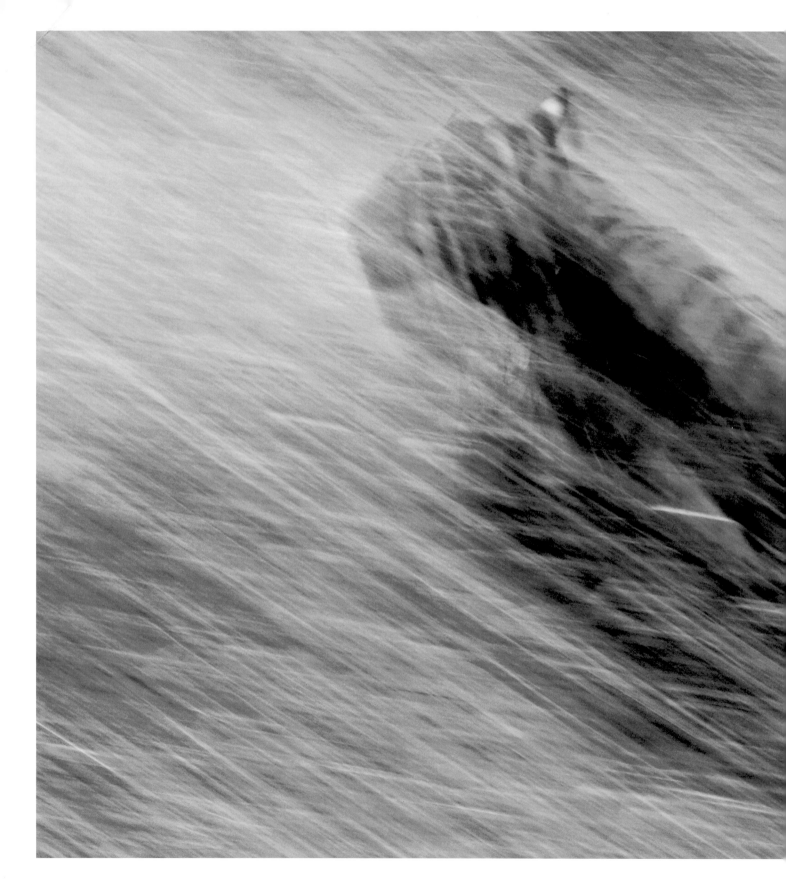

ON THE FRONTLINE:
INDIA

The tiger, national symbol of India, is under grave threat. And the situation is urgent: a 2008 census of India's tiger population showed numbers had halved in the previous five years.

While on assignment in India in 2008, I spoke to several villagers living close to Kanha National Park in Madhya Pradesh. Again and again I heard the same story, as told by the Kohka village Forest Committee: 'The government want us to protect the forest but they provide no support – financial, educational or otherwise – to help us in doing so. When we ask for help, government representatives come, they look around, they talk a lot, and then they go, never to be seen or heard from again. We are left to fend for ourselves and the only resource we have is the forest. What else are we to do?'

Compare India's approach to conservation with that of Rwanda (pages 84–85) and it is clear that the two are very different. In Rwanda, 76% of jobs related to tourism and the national park are held by inhabitants of the surrounding villages, giving the people most likely to be in conflict with the park a financial interest in protecting it. In India such jobs are filled by outsiders, with around just 1% of employees coming from the local villages. This gives the villagers no incentive to protect tigers and their habitat. Instead they see the forest as a resource for food and timber for both personal and commercial consumption. Poaching of tigers is rife, and animals that form the tigers' natural prey base are hunted for food. IUCN records these as two of the greatest current threats to the remaining tiger populations.

Of course poaching is illegal in India, but in practice there is little deterrent. Bail is typically granted where a suspect can prove ownership of land in the region. Land is cheap, so small pockets are bought by ringleaders and then doled out to captured poachers to secure their bail. The Forest Department responsible for the parks usually opposes bail, but its requests are often denied. A Forest Department official told me that corruption is the reason for these denials. Once released, poachers are relocated by their bosses and replacements drafted in from other regions: this is an organized operation. Even when convicted, poachers receive an average jail term of less than three years and often serve just a few months.

▶ *India's tiger population has halved in recent years, despite conservation groups receiving over US$40 million in contributions.*

◄ *The close proximity of human communities to tiger territory makes conflict inevitable.*

The tigers' declining prey base is another reason for human/tiger conflict, for it forces tigers to roam beyond the boundaries of the park in search of food. They often seize domestic cattle, leading villagers to set tiger traps in order to protect their livestock. In its defence, the government will point to compensation schemes set up to recompense farmers for livestock losses. However, bureaucracy and corruption burden these schemes and the cost to farmers in time and money usually far exceeds the value of the compensation awarded. One farmer in Kohka village told me of a claim he had made for the loss of four cows. These cows were worth 20,000 rupees; his award was half that value, took five months to process, and was only settled once a bribe had been paid to a government official.

Agricultural farmers are similarly left to fend for themselves. Whereas the national park in Rwanda is ringed by a dry-stone wall to prevent forest animals encroaching on neighbouring farmland and grazing on valuable crops, no such protection is afforded to the farmers in India. Wild animals are free to wander in and out of the park at will. To protect their crops and

their livelihoods, farmers lay snares in the buffer zone between the park and their lands. Like all snares these are indiscriminate and are as likely to trap tigers as deer and buffalo.

It is clear that there exists among the people of Rwanda and India two very different attitudes to their country's iconic wildlife. In Rwanda, the gorilla is seen as an asset, worth more to the country and its communities alive than dead. In India, despite its symbolic value, the tiger is seen by many people as a pest. In Rwanda, communities and government authorities are working together to do all they can to protect their natural assets. What I saw in India indicated the opposite: that villagers are in conflict with the government and wildlife authorities.

When assessing how the different attitudes affect conservation of tigers and gorillas, the numbers speak for themselves. In Rwanda, with the gorilla population steadily increasing, this magnificent ape has a good chance of survival. In India, as an outsider looking in, it is impossible to see any future for the tiger without a rapid and seismic change in political attitudes.

WILD ASIATIC WATER BUFFALO

Bubalus arnee
Endangered

The gravest threats to *Bubalus arnee* are interbreeding with feral and domestic buffalo, hunting and loss and degradation of habitat. Most of the species' former wetland habitat in the Indian subcontinent and Southeast Asia is now cultivated, and what remains is highly fragmented. However, there are vast tracts of suitable lowland forest from which the species has long since been hunted out, especially in Cambodia and Laos, and where reintroduction could be viable. Most populations still require protection from hunting, and an even greater priority is protection from contact with domestic bovines, especially domestic water buffalo.

▶ *Adult males form bachelor herds of up to ten individuals, with older males often solitary.*

▶▶ *Koshi Tappu Wildlife Reserve, where these images were taken, is home to the only remaining population of wild water buffalo in Nepal.*

▶▶ *Overleaf: Before their major population decline, wild buffalo were known to make long-distance seasonal migrations.*

SOUTHEAST ASIA & OCEANIA

This region, encompassing lands south of China and east of India, is of enormous importance to conservationists. It contains a large number of endangered terrestrial mammals, some 217 in total, including the Sumatran tiger, two subspecies of orangutan, the Asian elephant, two species of rhinoceros and a large percentage of the world's most endangered primates.

Southeast Asia is a particular focus, accounting for two-thirds of the total number of endangered mammal species across the region, nearly 90% of which live in forest habitat threatened by both deforestation for biological resource use and redevelopment of land for agriculture. Encroachment for other kinds of development is the next most serious threat. The threat from industries such as mining, primarily for coal, is also particularly high in Southeast Asia, affecting nearly one-fifth of endangered species. Modification of natural ecosystems and damage due to invasive species also score highly, while the number of species threatened by global warming is one of the highest of all regions.

In Oceania the story is similar. Around two-thirds of endangered mammals inhabit forests, with the remainder spread over all habitat types with the exception of desert. The most significant threat is redevelopment of land for agriculture, which affects almost half of endangered species, followed by invasive species, biological resource use and modification of natural ecosystems. As in Southeast Asia, global warming is a clear and present threat to endangered mammals in Oceania, affecting over 10% of the total.

One of the most talked-about threats to wildlife in this region is the expansion of the oil palm industry into forest and wetland areas. Indonesia and Malaysia dominate the global market for palm oil with projected output for 2008 reaching 19.7 million tonnes in Indonesia and 17.4 million in Malaysia. The industry is encouraged by governments keenly aware of the need to alleviate poverty and provide employment for large and rapidly increasing populations. In June 2008 the global market price for palm oil reached a value exceeding US$1,000 per tonne. In anyone's language that's a lot of money and, even though the price per tonne had dropped by September 2008 to around US$650, that still equates to an industry worth over US$24 billion, and one that is not simply going to go away.

I travelled to Borneo in April 2008 and on the flight between Kuala Lumpur and Kota Kinabalu I met Sarala Aikanathan, Director of the Malaysian branch of conservation NGO Wetlands International. She was on her way to the International Palm Oil Sustainability Conference organized by the Malaysian Palm Oil Council. I asked her what she was expecting of the conference. Her answer surprised me. She said that for many years the palm oil growers and conservationists had been like two boxers in a ring, hitting each other as hard as they could in the hope that the opposing side would fall down and not get up again. I agreed that this was a fair description of conservationist strategy in general in recent times.

Her belief, however, was that conservationists have come to realize that a sustainable palm oil industry is good for the people and the countries involved, and that the best way to conserve wildlife in Malaysia and Indonesia is to work with the industry to find a solution that suits both parties. Here, perhaps, is evidence of an emerging consensus that you can't beat the economic system around which all of our lives are entwined. If so, there may yet be some hope for species such as the orangutan and the tiger, and others less prominent in global consciousness but no less important to the ecological balance of the region and the ecological heritage of the planet.

NORTHERN WHITE-CHEEKED GIBBON

Nomascus leucogenys
Critically endangered

The northern white-cheeked gibbon occurs in Laos, Vietnam and, until recently, China. It has suffered from deforestation due to agricultural encroachment into mountainous areas, as well as fuel-wood and timber extraction from remaining forests, especially in China and Vietnam. Hunting for food, the pet trade and traditional medicine is a major threat throughout its range, and is the primary cause for the decline of the species in all three countries. Indeed it is now presumed extinct in China. It occurs in a mixture of protected areas and national parks throughout its range and is legally protected in Vietnam, though enforcement against forest encroachment and poaching is frequently inadequate.

◄ *White-cheeked gibbons exhibit a marked sexual dichromism. The male (far left) has coarse black body fur with white fur on his cheeks, while the female (left) is golden with a black face and dark brown or black fur on top of her head.*

LAR GIBBON

Hylobates lar
Endangered

The Lar gibbon is found in evergreen, semi-evergreen and mixed-evergreen deciduous forests in Thailand, Peninsular Malaysia and northern Sumatra, and is known to utilize regenerating secondary forests and selectively logged forests. The species' primary threat, overtaking forest clearance, is hunting, both for food and for the pet trade. Illegal use of forest products, as well as poaching, is common in most protected areas. Much of this hunting is by villagers, including within protected areas. Improved management and protection of existing reserves is needed urgently, ideally in ways that involve and benefit local communities.

◄ *Lar gibbons mature late, females at 8–10 years and males at 8–12 years, and have one offspring every 3–5 years.*

◄◄ *They use an elaborate system of calls and vocalizations to defend territories and keep track of family members.*

SILVERY JAVAN GIBBON

Hylobates moloch
Endangered

The historical deforestation that occurred across Java in colonial times has effectively restricted the silvery Javan gibbon to continuous tracts of forest around mountain and volcano tops. Although habitat loss continues, it is at a much slower rate today, and populations of gibbons, while isolated, are substantial in size and apparently stable. Hunting for the pet trade, however, exerts an as yet unquantified effect on the species.

◄ *The silvery Javan gibbon is strictly arboreal and eats mainly fruits as well as leaves and flowers.*

CELEBES CRESTED MACAQUE

Macaca nigra
Critically endangered

The Celebes crested macaque inhabits rainforest in the northeastern tip of Sulawesi and adjacent islands in Indonesia. It is threatened by habitat loss within its range as well as hunting for bushmeat and the illegal pet trade. Extensive illegal small-scale open-area mining for gold, using mercury, within protected areas is also a regional threat. Urgent action is needed to stop human encroachment into protected areas, especially Tangkoko, home to the most viable natural remaining population.

▶ *Birth of typically a single offspring happens in the spring when food is more plentiful. Young animals are nursed for around a year.*

▶▶ *This species is entirely black apart from its rump, which is a distinctive pink colour. In males this is small and heart-shaped, while in females it is large, rounded and a darker pink.*

▶▶ *Overleaf: The Celebes crested macaque eats mainly fruit but also immature leaves, arthropods, stalks of newly flowering plants and cultivated crops.*

RED-SHANKED DOUC LANGUR

Pygathrix nemaeus
Endangered

Hunting for meat, use in traditional medicine, and the pet trade is the primary threat to this species, which is found in parts of Vietnam, Cambodia and Laos. Habitat destruction also poses a significant threat: large parts of Vietnam have experienced substantial human population expansion in the postwar years, and there has been extensive logging and forest clearance for coffee, rubber and cashew plantations, as well as wood collecting. General infrastructure development, specifically the construction of the Ho Chi Minh Highway, also poses a major threat to habitat.

◄ *The red-shanked douc langur occurs in undisturbed primary and secondary evergreen and semi-evergreen broadleaf forests.*

BORNEAN ORANGUTAN

Pongo pygmaeus
Endangered

The population of Bornean orangutans is estimated to be less than 14% of what it was in the mid-20th century. Vast areas of the species' forest habitat have been lost through legal and illegal logging and clearance for agriculture and oil palm plantations. Massive forest fires have also taken a major toll, and hunting for bushmeat, the pet trade and to protect crops is a serious threat in parts of the island. Although some major populations are found within the network of protected forests, the majority of Bornean orangutans live outside these areas. New mechanisms to ensure their long-term survival are urgently needed.

◄   To protect baby orangutans,
     mothers will deposit
     them in high branches,
     returning later when
     the threat has gone.

◄◄ More than 500 plant species
     have been recorded in the
     orangutan's diet, over 60%
     of which is made up of fruit.

►► Overleaf: Baby orangutans
     stay with their mothers
     for around 6–7 years.

ON THE FRONTLINE:
BORNEO

Lias bin Barapa's father died when Lias was a teenager, back in 1959. With no one else in the family to support them, Lias left school to find a job. In the village where he lived his options were limited, a choice between labouring on a farm, fishing or resin harvesting. None of these appealed; he wanted to do something different. There was a new logging company in the area that was recruiting, and so Lias signed up and went to work in the timber industry for the equivalent in today's money of US$45 per month.

That was enough to pay the rent on the family home and buy the necessary provisions that couldn't be caught in the Kinabatangan River, such as rice, sugar, salt and tinned foods, which were ferried from Sandakan twice a month. But the work was hard and dangerous. In those days there were no chainsaws or machinery. Trees were chopped by axe and then hauled through the forest with ropes. Often workers' feet would become tangled in the ropes, as the enormous logs rolled down the hillside. 'There were many accidents ... deaths,' Lias told me.

But in those pre-mechanical days, logging was sustainable, the company felling perhaps just seven or eight trees per day. 'This was important,' Lias told

me, 'because the forest was part of our home.' I asked him how often he would see orangutans and proboscis monkeys – two of the area's now endangered species. 'All the time,' he said. 'But no one disturbed them and they were happy to live around us.'

Then, in the mid-1960s, chainsaws and tractors were introduced. Felling became more intensive and clear-felling (where every tree in a harvested area is cut down) became standard practice. To help with the increased workload, the logging company brought in workers from Indonesia and Sarawak. These migrant labourers were cheaper to employ but they cared nothing for the forest. As they took more and more of the jobs, opportunities for locals dwindled. With the logging company unwilling to pay higher rates to local workers, unemployment became rife and the village's economy declined. And, as the forests disappeared, so too did the wildlife.

By the 1980s Lias was married and had a family of his own. He had been lucky and had kept his job, earning enough to buy his own home, but he was now getting too old and tired to continue. Eventually he got a job with the government, working as a boatman. The money wasn't as

► *Borneo's rainforests are being cleared to make way for more financially productive oil palm plantations.*

good but the work was less strenuous and, in his spare time, he began to farm the small parcel of land around his house to supplement his income.

In 1994, in an effort to diversify the economy, the government introduced an incentive for landowners to grow ginger. Lias saw an opportunity to take control of his family's destiny. He dreamed of building a small business that would provide a future for his children and grandchildren. It would be his legacy. He worked hard for nine months, planting *Zingiber officinale* and harvesting the roots from which ginger spice comes. For his efforts he earned just 15 ringgits – about US$4 in today's money. The venture almost ruined his family.

Three years later, in 1997, the Malaysian Department for Agriculture launched another initiative, this time to encourage landowners to cultivate palm plantations for palm oil. After the ginger debacle, Lias was wary of government initiatives, but with no other work available – even fishing was no longer an option as the river had become polluted by the logging and milling companies – he signed up. To qualify for the government subsidy, Lias had to sign over the title to his land. In essence, the 'subsidy' was little more than a loan secured on his home, the same as a mortgage. He is paying back the loan, interest free, and hopes to one day get back his deeds so that he can pass on the home to his children when he dies.

Lias is now in his 70s. He is still working on his smallholding, although his second-eldest son, Jamal, runs the operation. I asked him how he feels about the life he has led and what he has achieved. 'What else is

◀ Bornean orangutan populations are restricted to isolated patches of forest and their numbers are declining.

there but to provide for your family and leave something behind for them?' he replied.

I also asked him his views on the impact logging and the palm oil industry have had on his country's natural resources and its wildlife.

'I have worked hard doing manual labour for over fifty years. I have never had more than I needed at any one time, just enough to feed and house my family. You do what you must to survive with the resources you have. It is the same for most people in Borneo. It is the same for the government. Logging and the palm oil industry are simply ways for the government to earn the country's living from the resources it has.

'If the world wants to save our forests and our wildlife, then it must help us develop new ways of earning a living. It is not that we don't appreciate nature, or that we don't care about conservation. But when you are living hand to mouth, as I have done all my life, and as this country is doing today, conservation is a luxury that only the rich can afford.'

PROBOSCIS MONKEY

Nasalis larvatus
Endangered

Proboscis monkeys are native to Borneo, mainly inhabiting lowland coastal and riverine forest (including mangroves), peat and freshwater swamp forest. These habitats are ideal for logging, cultivation and settlement, and consequently the major cause for the species' decline is habitat destruction. Proboscis monkeys are lethargic animals, easily hunted; with little effort entire populations can be wiped out. Opportunistic hunting for food occurs but the species is also hunted for intestinal bezoar stones, an ingredient in traditional Chinese medicine. It is protected by law throughout its range, but enforcement in some areas suffers from governmental and institutional deficiencies, including lack of conservation funds and knowledge.

◀ *The bulbous nose, unique among primates, measures up to 18 cm (7 in) long and is only seen on males.*

◀◀ *Proboscis monkeys are agile creatures able to leap great distances.*

▶▶ *Overleaf: Babies travel with the mother, carried on her hip or, when necessary, clinging to her underbelly.*

BORNEO BAY CAT

Pardofelis badia
Endangered

The Borneo bay cat is forest-dependent, and the species' major threat is habitat loss due to commercial logging and forest clearance for oil palm plantations. If deforestation continues at current rates, forest cover on the island of Borneo is projected to decline from half to less than a third by 2020. Oil palm plantations in particular are likely to expand in the future as a result of the international push for biofuels. Wildlife traders, aware of the bay cat's rarity, hunt it for the skin and pet markets, even though the species is protected by national legislation across most of its range.

◄   The Borneo bay cat is
    found only in forested
    areas on the island Borneo.
    It is extremely rare and
    secretive, and its distribution
    remains poorly known.

SUMATRAN RHINOCEROS

Dicerorhinus sumatrensis
Critically endangered

The notoriously shy Sumatran rhinoceros is dependent on salt licks and occurs mainly in hilly forested areas, close to water sources. Its two principal threats are poaching and reduced population viability. Hunting is primarily driven by the demand for horns and other body parts, which are believed to have medicinal properties. The species is now so reduced that it survives only in small numbers in isolated pockets. The total population is estimated at fewer than 275 individuals. Consequently, breeding activity is infrequent, successful births are uncommon and there is a severe risk of inbreeding depression. The expansion and reinforcement of successful anti-poaching programmes is a top priority if the species is to survive.

◄ *The movement of rhinoceroses between feeding sites and wallows is at most a few kilometres per day.*

►► *Overleaf: The species is generally solitary, apart from mating pairs and mothers with their young.*

JAVAN RHINOCEROS

Rhinoceros sondaicus
Critically endangered

The last surviving population of Javan rhinoceroses, an estimated 40–60 animals, lives in Ujung Kulon National Park, on Java's western tip. Another, very small, population occurs in the Cat Tien National Park in southern Vietnam, with as few as six individuals remaining. There are no animals currently in captivity. The species' decline is mainly attributable to poaching to meet the demand for rhino horn and other products used in Chinese and related medicine. A Rhino Protection Unit has been established on Java and there is an urgent need to consider the feasibility of a reintroduction or translocation programme in Cat Tien.

◄ *Javan rhinoceroses sometimes congregate at salt licks and mud wallows, but are generally solitary. Because of their extreme rarity, however, relatively little is known about their biology and preferred habitat.*

SUMATRAN ORANGUTAN

Pongo abelii
Critically endangered

The population of Sumatran orangutans has declined by 80% in 75 years. The majority today live in the province of Aceh, at the northern tip of Sumatra. Most exist outside protected areas in forests that are threatened by logging (both legal and illegal), particularly as a result of dramatically increased demand for timber and other natural resources after the 2004 tsunami. The species is also seriously threatened by wholesale conversion of forest to agricultural land and oil palm plantations, and fragmentation of forest areas by roads.

▶ *With their forests fast disappearing, orangutans urgently need our help.*

▶▶ *According to some biologists, orangutan babies need love almost as much as they need nourishment in order to survive.*

▶▶ *Overleaf: The long-term future of the Sumatran orangutan is uncertain. Even selective logging in its ranges causes numbers to plummet by up to 60%.*

PREVENTION RATHER THAN CURE

Before I became a wildlife photojournalist, I used to work in IT sales. During that time, I was sent on a variety of training courses, one of which focused on time management. Now time is something I never seem to have enough of, perhaps precisely because time management has never been my strong point. However, one thing I took away from this particular course was a simple method of organizing a to-do list.

The advice was as follows: anything that arrives on your desk should be assigned to one of three boxes: 1) neither urgent nor important; 2) important; or 3) urgent. The theory goes that if you do all the things in the important box in a timely manner, nothing on your to-do list will ever make its way to becoming urgent. (Anything marked neither urgent nor important should go straight in the bin.)

I relate this story because it explains the point of this short chapter. For while the scope of this book has been to focus primarily on those species classified as Endangered and Critically Endangered, there is a third category that is applied to species under threat: Vulnerable.

For a species to be included in any of these categories it must satisfy a carefully defined set of criteria that are designed to enable an objective and easily understood assessment of its risk of extinction. At the same time, IUCN acknowledges that 'although the system places species into the threatened categories with a high degree of consistency, the criteria do not take into account the life histories of every species. Hence, in certain individual cases, the risk of extinction may be under- or over-estimated.'

In part, this explains the absence of certain species that one might have expected to find in this book. Indeed, part of the personal journey I have undertaken has been not so much the discovery of which mammals are included on the list as Endangered and Critically Endangered, but those that are not ... yet.

These pages feature five species classed as Vulnerable on the IUCN Red List of Threatened Species™. Four of them one might have expected to find in *Animals on the Edge*, while one – the common hippopotamus – may come as a surprise. There are many more that could equally well have appeared here. For although animals classed as Endangered and Critically Endangered clearly demand our urgent attention, there are many others for which taking action now is vital if we are to avoid them too becoming an urgent priority within a generation.

POLAR BEAR *Ursus maritimus*

Polar bears rely almost exclusively on the Arctic marine sea-ice environment for their survival, to the extent that large-scale changes in their habitat will have a negative impact on the global population. Such a threat is posed by climate change. Recent modelling of sea-ice trends predicts dramatic reductions in coverage over the next 50–100 years. And while bear species in general show adaptability in dealing with their surroundings and habitat, polar bears are highly specialized in their adaptation to life in the Arctic marine environment. Furthermore, they exhibit low reproductive rates with long generational spans. Together, these factors make it less likely that polar bears will be able to adapt successfully to a changed environment.

There is little doubt that polar bears will have a lesser habitat quality in the future. Some have speculated that the species might become extinct within a hundred years, with a population decrease of more than 50% in the next 45 years; but it is believed that a more realistic evaluation proposes a reduction of 30% in that period, which meets the criteria for an assessment of Vulnerable on the IUCN Red List.

◀ *A forecast reduction of 30% over the next 45 years means the polar bear is classed as Vulnerable by IUCN.*

CHEETAH *Acinonyx jubatus*

The known cheetah population is not much greater than 7,000 mature individuals, and it is believed that the total population is unlikely to exceed 10,000. These figures are at a level consistent with the criteria that place the species in the Vulnerable category on the IUCN Red List.

While the current rate of population decline is of most concern, and the historical rate of decline has been severe, attention has also focused on the possibility that the species suffered even more extreme losses in the distant past, which may account for the remarkably low level of genetic diversity in comparison with other big cats, such as lions, tigers and leopards. This lack of genetic diversity suggests inbreeding among a very few individuals that survived one or more catastrophic population bottlenecks in the past, with the first possibly occurring during the late Pleistocene extinctions around 10,000 years ago.

While the causes of the cheetah's low levels of genetic variation are unclear, the consequence is that large populations are necessary to conserve the species. And, since cheetahs are a low-density species, protected areas need to be larger than average for conservation efforts to be successful.

► Cheetahs have disappeared from 76% of their historic range in Africa, while in Asia there now exists only a tiny sub-population of 60–100 individuals in Iran.

◀ *Lions are found in most countries in sub-Saharan Africa, though the species' status is unknown across large parts of its range.*

LION *Panthera leo*

Estimating the size of the African lion population is an ambitious and uncertain exercise. However, a species population reduction of approximately 30% is suspected over the past two decades, leading to its classification as Vulnerable.

The main cause of this decline is killing in defence of human life and livestock, and this is unlikely to have ceased. It is estimated that lions cost ranchers living alongside Tsavo East National Park in Kenya US$290 per year in livestock losses. Likewise, annual losses of cattle in areas adjacent to Waza National Park in Cameroon,

while comprising only about 3.1% of all livestock losses, are estimated to represent more than 22% of financial losses, amounting to about US$370 per owner. These figures are very significant: in their respective countries, they equate to the annual salary of an employee. As a consequence, lions are persecuted intensively in livestock areas across Africa. Implementation of appropriate livestock management measures, coupled with problem animal control measures and mechanisms for compensating livestock losses, are among the primary responses needed to resolve human/lion conflict.

▶ *The clouded leopard's forest habitat is fast disappearing, and illegal hunting has been prolific in recent times.*

CLOUDED LEOPARD *Neofelis nebulosa*

The clouded leopard is found from the Himalayan foothills in Nepal through mainland Southeast Asia into China. It is forest-dependent, being strongly associated with primary evergreen tropical rainforest, dry and deciduous forest and secondary and logged forests. However, its traditional habitat is being destroyed by logging and conversion at a rate greater than any other in the world today, putting pressure on surviving populations throughout its range. It is also widely hunted. Market surveys have identified large numbers of skins and there is known to be illegal trade in bones for medicines, meat for exotic dishes and live animals for the pet trade. Its total effective population size is suspected to be fewer than 10,000 mature individuals, with no single population numbering more than 1,000, placing the species in the Vulnerable category on the IUCN Red List.

HIPPOPOTAMUS *Hippopotamus amphibius*

While the previous four species in the Vulnerable category were perhaps predictable, the inclusion of the common hippopotamus may come as a surprise to many. The 1996 IUCN assessment described hippopotamus populations as 'widespread and secure'. Since then, however, there have been substantial changes in several key countries in the species' range. An extreme example is the Democratic Republic of Congo, which has seen a decline in numbers exceeding 95% as a result of intense hunting pressure during more than eight years of civil unrest and conflict. The most recent population estimates suggest that over the past ten years there has been a 7–20% decline in overall hippopotamus populations and it is believed likely that this will exceed 30% over the next three generations (30 years).

The causes of this decline include illegal and unregulated hunting for meat and ivory (found in the teeth), and habitat loss resulting from water diversion for agricultural development, as well as larger-scale development in and around wetland areas. Such threats have not diminished, nor is there evidence they will do so in the near future.

◄ *Common hippos are found in many countries throughout sub-Saharan Africa, but have suffered a serious decline in numbers in the last ten years.*

ON ASSIGNMENT:
A PHOTOGRAPHER'S JOURNAL

▶ *A silver langur takes an interest in my remote camera set-up. Sabah, Borneo.*

Fans of wildlife photography can view images in books, magazines, exhibitions or online. But rarely do they have chance to glimpse the events that make these images possible – to follow the photographer on the adventure from initial concept to finished work. Throughout his assignments for *Animals on the Edge* Chris Weston kept a diary, recording many memorable moments in the field. What follows are extracts from his journal of 2008, the year that most of the images in this book were shot.

INDIA *January 2008*

The plane touches down in Delhi early in the morning. I cross to the domestic terminal in a rickety old bus and then settle in for an eight-hour wait before my flight to Nagpur, where I meet my guides and tiger consultants, Nanda Rana and Latika Nath Rana. Together we set out in 4×4s on a five-hour drive through the night to our camp near Kanha National Park.

Just three hours after arriving at camp, we are up again and heading into the park. On the way, Nanda collects our special permits, required for the off-limits access I need for my photography. Only much later does he confess to me that these only turned up the night before, delayed by government bureaucracy, despite a formal application several weeks in advance. Without them my journey would have been a wasted one.

In the park, we stop off at one of the forest stations and are told of a nearby sighting. This sounds promising. We head on to pick up the elephants we'll be using to track the tigers. This is my first experience of photographing on elephant-back. It feels a bit like being in a small boat on a gentle swell. But I soon get the hang of it: the pachyderm proves a very stable platform.

Just five minutes into our expedition I catch my first ever glimpse of a wild tiger. He is a young, solitary male, probably in his first year away from the protective custody of his mother. He is initially nervous but we stay back until he settles, and then we follow him, first across open grasslands and then on into the forest. We remain with him into the failing light and that evening I shoot some of my best images of the entire trip.

The next day, another early start and we are back on the elephants. The terrain is more difficult. There are no paths through the forest and more than once we come to what appears to be an impenetrable cluster of trees and thicket. A shouted command from the mahout, however, and the elephant uses its powerful trunk to break through

with apparent ease, opening up a new track into the interior. But despite our persistence and the skill of the mahouts, tigers evade us. Apart from a fleeting glimpse of a leopard, late in the afternoon, the day is a washout as far as photography is concerned.

This proves to be the pattern of my time in India: sightings one day, nothing the next. But over the course of my stay I encounter nine different individuals, including a mother with three young cubs, and enjoy some of the most inspiring wildlife encounters of my career. It's a great start to the project.

BORNEO *March 2008*

Shortly after returning from India, I am repacking my gear and heading to the forests of Borneo. The focus of this trip is the *Nasalis larvatus*, the proboscis or long-nosed monkey – distinctive because of the male's large, bulbous, protruding snout. Proboscis monkeys are endemic to Borneo's low-elevation mangrove forests and lowland riverside forests. Like the island's other iconic primate, the orangutan, they spend most of their lives in

◀ *Elephants were a regular form of transport during my quest to photograph endangered species, as here in Nepal.*

trees, making them difficult to photograph at the best of times. To complicate matters, I am attempting a unique shot: I want to photograph a male leaping between trees, directly towards the camera.

At the airport I meet my guide for the assignment, Cede Prudente. Cede is a well-known photographer in his own right, and a respected travel operator in Malaysian Borneo. We quickly go over the assignment before heading to camp. The plan is two-fold: first we will set up remote cameras at Labuk Bay before heading deeper into the forest and the Kinabatangan River, an area rich in wildlife and one of the last remaining wild habitats where proboscis monkeys and orangutans thrive.

At camp I test all the electronic equipment before storing it in a separate room without air conditioning. Heat and humidity are a major challenge to the photographer in the tropics. Air conditioning might make things more comfortable for humans, but taking camera equipment from a cool environment directly into the jungle will cause moisture to form on lens elements and the camera interior: not good.

In the morning we begin setting up the camera traps. I have identified a position where a group of bachelor males visit regularly. I fix my cameras to tripods that are disguised to blend with the surroundings. To activate the shutters I am using infrared remote triggers that I will fire manually from a distant, concealed position. I fire off a few test shots to make certain that the remote triggers work, and that there are no obstacles that will interfere with the transmission between trigger and camera.

Once I am satisfied I enter my blind and wait ... and

wait. It is 30 degrees Celsius (86 Fahrenheit) in the shade and close to 100% humidity. After a few hours I am very ready to leave ... cue the arrival of the group of males in the trees around me.

With the low light levels and my need for a fast shutter speed, the technology provided by my latest digital camera proves a real blessing. The ability to shoot at relatively high ISO values, without having to worry about degrading image quality, means I am able to freeze the motion of the monkeys as they leap. Knowing when to trigger the shutter comes down to my close observation of the creatures and their body language, all the while taking account of the short delay between the transmission and arrival of the infrared signal.

The set-up is working well until a langur takes a close interest in my cameras and starts taking its own pictures.

▶ Me searching for orangutans
from the Kinabatangan
River, Borneo.

Nonetheless, by the end of the day the shots are in the bag, and I head for the Kinabatangan River in search of the more elusive orangutan. I have a feeling that things are about to get harder.

SUMATRA *April 2008*

After several unproductive days by the Kinabatangan River, I leave Borneo and head to the Indonesian island of Sumatra to photograph the critically endangered Sumatran orangutan. On a map it looks like a quick hop across the water, but my journey involves three flights and an overnight stop in Kuala Lumpur en route to the northern city of Medan. There I will meet up with my guide in a suitable 4×4 and drive the five hours to Gunung Leuser National Park.

That is the plan. There is just one problem ... no guide and no car. After waiting an hour I take matters into my own hands and hire a taxi. The driver is willing, but I soon see why the original plan included a 4×4 as the city roads give way to broken tarmac that, in places, drops a foot between one section and the next where monsoon rains have swept away much of the road's construction. We arrive bumped, battered and very tired. The taxi driver

◀ *Darma Budi, our forest guide, looks for signs of orangutans. Gunung Leuser National Park, Sumatra.*

turns back, wearily shaking his head, wondering how much new suspension rods are going to cost him.

In camp I am united with my guide and the next morning we head into the park, initially to meet with Forest Department officials before heading off in search of orangutans. The route involves a 15-minute walk along the riverbank and a precarious river crossing in a dugout canoe. Once across the river, we hike up into the forest to a feeding platform that has been set up to help orphaned apes that have been rehabilitated and reintroduced into the wild. Although the position of the platform provides few photographic opportunities, it gives me a chance to familiarize myself with the habitat and behaviour of my subject.

I have several ideas in mind for photographs. I am keen to use my newly acquired fish-eye lens. I also want to photograph the dominant male in the area, whose strong facial features and giant size make him one of the species' most valued individuals. He has been proving elusive, but my Forest Department guide is confident that we will find him during one of our treks deep into the jungle.

Next morning we set off early, led by the forest ranger and with a porter to help carry the equipment, on what proves a long day in sweltering temperatures and high humidity. The orangutans are wary of humans, their confidence battered after years of illegal hunting. Throughout the day we see solitary individuals high up in

◀ *My guide, Sabarata, sits up front as we head back to camp after a long day tracking orangutans. Gunung Leuser National Park, Sumatra.*

the canopy. I shoot some images including, towards evening, a beautiful silhouette. But there is no chance to use the fish-eye lens and no sign of the big male.

A few days later our luck changes. Dusk is closing in when our spotter points skyward to a shape high up in the canopy, moving easily between the trees – it is the large male. There is little light and the forest canopy makes composing images difficult, but for a brief, fleeting moment, as he passes overhead between two trees, he seems to stop, suspended almost in mid-air, giving me a perfect silhouette and one of my favourite images from the entire shoot.

Shortly after that day, at breakfast one morning, we receive news from the Forest Department that shatters our morale. The male has been found, barely alive, with

▶ *Crossing the river to enter Gunung Leuser National Park, Sumatra, in search of orangutans.*

▶ *Photographing a mother and baby orangutan. Gunung Leuser National Park, Sumatra.*

▶▶ *An orangutan silhouetted against the sky at dusk. Gunung Leuser National Park, Sumatra.*

26 air gun pellets embedded in his head and body. He is in the local veterinary clinic on life support and the prognosis is not good. We eat our rice breakfast and head back into the forest, but my heart isn't in it and the forest ranger, usually so upbeat, is mute and lethargic. There is little point continuing the shoot so we head back early and wait for an update on the orangutan's health. The news comes later that night. The male is dead.

I have three more days in Sumatra, which we spend trekking in the forest, in search of more orangutans. Photographically, this assignment has been a great success. But I will always remember it for the meaningless death of the dominant male orangutan. One of the main aims of this project is to try and gain an understanding of the motives behind actions that imperil wildlife. Sometimes, however, there simply is no rhyme or reason.

NEPAL *May 2008*

After a much needed rest, the next stop on my global quest is Nepal, another country I have never visited before. Having negotiated my way through customs, I am met by my good friend Nanda Rana, a Nepali himself, who worked with me in India at the beginning of the year.

First on my list of species is the greater one-horned rhinoceros, which Nanda has been researching on my behalf since India. Until recently, Nepal had a population of around 500 rhinos but their number halved during the insurgency of 2003–7 and once again this great creature is close to extinction.

To track the rhinos, we again take to elephant-back. After my Indian adventure I am quickly in the swing of things and, for the next three days, we crash through the

► Our mahout guides
his elephant while
tracking rhinos. Chitwan
National Park, Nepal.

forest, stumble across grasslands and wade through rivers in our search for this elusive creature. Occasionally we see one cutting through the grassy plains like a mower across a lawn, or lolling in the cooling water of a river or pond. At one point, we come across a mother shielding an inquisitive calf, whose stumpy-nosed head, yet to grow its prominent horn, peers around a bush to check us out.

All the time I keep the camera clicking but, in truth, so far I only have a single shot that I am really happy with. The others are all good material for the picture library, documenting behaviour and habitat, but I want more, something different. It's time for a change of strategy.

The next day Nanda and I decide to track a single rhino for as long as it remains undisturbed by our presence. Being on elephants is a help. Our rhino spends much of the day ignoring us, giving me time to get a much better handle on its habits. I leave Chitwan satisfied that the images are in the bag.

► Exhausted at the end of a
strenuous day in the field.
The sign on the Land Rover
advises insurgents that
we are non-military and
not a target. Koshi Tappu
Wildlife Reserve, Nepal.

From Chitwan we head across country to Koshi Tappu Wildlife Reserve, on what turns out to be the proverbial road to hell. It starts well enough, with

a stop in Bharatpur for a meeting with the head of police to progress my request to interview convicted wildlife poachers. It is after Bharatpur that the fun begins. First, a student protest blocks the main road – the only road – out towards Koshi. We find a way around, cutting through farm tracks and what seem to be private driveways. But even when we finally do make it back onto the road, we are slowed by a constant stream of people, cattle, bicycles, goats, pedestrians, chickens and ... well, more people. In what appears to be a mass suicide attempt, anyone and everything with legs or wheels constantly steps or rides directly in front of our car when we least expect it and, frankly, when it is least advisable to do so.

The only defence against this assault is the car's horn. And so for the duration of the nine-hour trip our driver toots the horn every few seconds. For the first few miles, this is tolerable, but it isn't long before it begins to feel like the bells of Big Ben ringing inside my head. It is over 34 degrees Celsius (93 Fahrenheit) but the driver refuses to turn on the air conditioning because there is a severe fuel shortage in Nepal. On top of all this I am subjected to his favourite CD, which, it transpires, is a collection of soundtracks from Nepal's most popular TV adverts. Every so often I ask him to turn it off, but my pleas obviously get lost in translation, as each time he smiles at me, nods and turns the volume even louder. All the while, Nanda sleeps happily, his face under his hat, sprawled across the rear seat.

Finally, as the sun begins to set, and after I have shed several pounds and most of my clothes, we come to a sign that reads 'Koshi Tappu Wildlife Reserve, 2.6 km'. Almost there, I cheer to myself. An hour later we find the camp, along a completely different, unsigned road. I head straight for bed.

I awake with renewed energy and enthusiasm. I have come to Koshi Tappu to photograph the endangered wild Asiatic buffalo. We have a meeting first thing with the park warden to ask permission to enter some of the restricted areas. This takes over an hour, simply because that's the way things are done in Nepal, but, mellowed by a pot of hot tea, he agrees to our request.

We plan to use river rafts to find the herds before heading out on foot with the cameras. But it quickly becomes apparent that we are going to need back-up. The buffalo are incredibly wary and, having strong senses of smell and hearing, they run at the very first sign of us. Then, when they are several hundred metres away, they run some more. It proves impossible to get within 200 metres before they hightail it across the plains.

That evening we head to the local village and recruit a team of what I nickname 'buffalo soldiers'. The plan is to set up a blind behind the buffalo, from where I will take the photographs. The buffalo soldiers will circle around to a position behind the herd. From there, they will emerge, making themselves visible in the hope that the herd will turn and retreat, charging directly towards me. For the buffalo soldiers it is hard and at times dangerous work in difficult terrain with uncooperative subjects. Three quit during the assignment, but the rest stay on to complete the job. Thanks to their invaluable help, I leave Nepal with a great set of images.

RWANDA *June 2008*

Having spent much of the first part of 2008 in the steamy jungles of Asia, it is a relief that my next assignment is taking me back to Africa to track mountain gorillas in the Virunga Mountains. Rwanda is one of my favourite African countries. Its people are generous and welcoming, and proud of the achievements they have made since the horrors of 1994, including their country's increasing population of mountain gorillas.

My assignment begins in one of the communities on the edge of the forest, where I interview villagers and community leaders before heading off into the dense forest for my first trek. The walk to the gorillas is arduous. Late, heavy rains have left the ground sodden and, in places, slippery as ice. The pathways up the mountain have frequently become overgrown and we have to cut a

◄ *Porters from a local village help to release our 4x4 after it got bogged down in the mud. Volcanoes National Park, Rwanda.*

route through the trees with machetes. It is three hard hours before we finally meet up with the guards who protect the gorillas and who have talked us in using two-way radios. According to my GPS we are nearly 2,750 metres (9,000 feet) above sea level.

The presence of the guards indicates that the gorillas are now very near and a further short walk takes us into an open clearing where we encounter the Sousa group, the largest gorilla band visited by tour groups, with around 40 members, including three silverbacks and the species' only known surviving twins. I first saw these four years ago, when they were less than a year old. It is a thrill to see them now, independent, strong and healthy.

All gorillas in a band, including the males and teenagers, play a part in raising baby gorillas. A dominant silverback can often be seen cradling a baby in his gigantic arms, grooming and playing with it, and teaching it the ways of the world. As our gorillas shift position and we jostle out of their way, a machete that a guide has stabbed into the ground becomes abandoned. A baby gorilla spies the tool and shuffles over to it, trying to appear nonchalant. From the corner of his eye, however, a silverback is watching him. As the baby reaches out to grab the machete, the silverback knocks his hand away with a soft punch that sends the toddler rolling into a bush, leaving him in no doubt that this is no plaything. After that, the baby leaves the machete well alone.

On our last trek, on my fourth day in the country, we set out as usual, this time heading to a smaller group of gorillas. The weather is cold and overcast, and the terrain difficult. After a long hike, we finally arrive at a clearing on a steep side of the mountain. We have been here a short while, moving slowly with the gorillas as they make their way across the clearing, when I notice a female sitting alone, apart from the main group. I point her out to one of the guides and the two of us move towards her, careful not to intrude too closely. As we get nearer, we notice something moving in her arms. Our pulses begin to race in anticipation.

Then the guide looks at me and smiles broadly, making a cradling gesture with his arms. A few more steps, and we see. The female is nursing a newborn baby. We are as close as feels comfortable, so we crouch to observe her. The new mother watches us, still feeding her baby. Then, after a brief time, she shifts her position and opens her arms, revealing to us her son. He is less than ten days old and we are the first humans ever to see him. I take a photograph and then stop. There are some rare moments in the field to which no picture will ever do justice – this is one of them.

CONGO AND CENTRAL AFRICAN REPUBLIC *September 2008*

This is my first experience of central Africa, a region that to many is the continent's true heart. My ground agent tried his best to prepare me: long journeys from A to B, backwards systems, extremely basic amenities and a propensity for things not to work are all highlighted in bold on the travel information sheet. Within 24 hours of being on the ground in Congo I find out for myself exactly what I am in for.

I rise early to catch the internal flight from Brazzaville to Ouésso, where I am to meet up with the transport that will take me further north into the jungles of the Central African Republic (CAR) and Bai Hokou Research Camp, where I will be tracking lowland gorillas. That, at least, is the plan. The aircraft doesn't turn up. Jerry, my guide for the assignment, goes off to investigate. He reappears several hours later with the news that the flight is cancelled and that we are switching to plan B. 'What's plan B?' I ask. 'I don't know,' Jerry replies, 'I haven't figured it out yet.'

Plan B, it transpires, involves waiting a day in Brazzaville and catching a different flight the next morning. My schedule is already tight and the delay is not going to help. Fortunately, next morning we have better luck and the plane arrives.

We land in Ouésso and head for the

Sangha River, a tributary of the mighty Congo River, where our boat awaits. It is a pirogue, a simple hollowed-out tree trunk with an engine hung off the back. We load the gear and settle in for the long journey north. After four hours we arrive at a World Conservation Society camp in Bomassa. Our plan is to continue on to Bayanga but it is late and the river is no place to be after dark. We bed down for the night.

We reach Bayanga the following afternoon, crossing the Congo/CAR border without incident. Grabbing the cameras, we immediately set off to Dzangha Bai. A bai is a natural forest clearing where animals come to feed on the soil's rich mineral salts. After an hour-long trek, much of it through swollen rivers, we reach the clearing. I am hoping to see gorillas but none are about. However, I am greeted by a large herd of forest elephants, a breathtaking sight, and I stay at the bai for the rest of the day.

The following day, we set off in search of the lowland gorillas, led by pygmy trackers from the Ba'Aka tribe. To them the forest is spiritual, and I watch with immense respect as they 'read' their way to the gorillas. During a break in the trek, I ask whether they feel they receive any benefit from the conservation work that is carried out in the forest. The response tells a familiar story.

'Conservationists take from the forest what benefits them but give nothing back to the people who live here,' one of them tells me. I ask what he means. 'Our people have been taking care of this forest for centuries. We know it; it is our home. When conservation groups come, they fight for laws that restrict our way of life, then they employ outsiders to work in the forest, leaving us with very little.'

We walk on. After a while, I begin to hear the sounds of the gorillas around me: dry leaves crackling under

► *Google Earth satellite image showing my location for photographing gorillas in Congo.*

soft footsteps, the gentle snapping of branches and the odd low guttural grunt. Here there are no clearings. We are surrounded by shadowy forest and among the trees dark shapes move. A tracker points to a gap between two trunks and there, sitting nonchalantly, is a big silverback.

My camera is in hand, but at first I just sit and observe him. He notices me and for a moment our eyes meet. I consider lifting the camera but something stops me; maybe I am awaiting his permission. He looks away from me and around him, scouting to see where the rest of his group are. Then he goes back to picking grubs from the earth. It is a sign that he is comfortable with my presence. He is allowing me to continue.

Time with the gorillas is restricted and over two days I get to spend just two hours with them. Too soon, we are returning south to Congo to look for a second group. Back in the pirogue, we set off down the river. It is raining heavily and I am wearing my waterproof jacket, picked up in the outdoor clothing store in my local high street. It has a camouflage pattern; it was all they had in stock. I am about to wish I'd gone to another store.

We arrive at the border and moor the pirogue. Then Jerry sets off to get our passports stamped and the boatman disappears for a break. I am in the boat alone when a border security policeman passes. Suddenly he stops, shouts something and raises his rifle, an AK-47. I hold out my hands in a submissive gesture and, like a typical Brit in a foreign country, say, 'I don't speak ...' I don't speak what? I am not sure what language he is speaking. But nor does he speak English, so it doesn't really matter.

I sit tight and nervously wait for Jerry who, noticing the confrontation, returns with several other policemen in tow. There is some heated debate and a lot of hand gesturing before all goes quiet. The AK-47-wielding policeman comes over to me, reaches down and offers me his hand. He then says something I don't understand but, as he is smiling, I shake his hand and thank him, in English. He departs and Jerry returns to the boat.

◄ *Clearing a fallen tree from the track. Bai Hokou, Congo.*

'What was all that about?' I ask. 'He thought that because you were wearing a military-style jacket, you were army personnel,' he replies. 'And what did he just say to me?' I ask again. 'He said he hopes your book is a success,' Jerry grins.

We travel on into Congo and camp the night in Bomassa. The next day we set off for the research centre at Mondika. The journey involves a long 4×4 drive as far into the forest as the road will take us, followed by a three-hour hike to camp. About half-way into the drive, a fallen tree blocks our path and we have to cut our way through. We finally clear a path and set off again. Around the next bend, a much larger tree has fallen and this time there is no way we are going to get through. We hump the bags of equipment and provisions onto our backs and set off on foot – 8 km (5 miles) sooner than expected.

The trek through the forest is gruelling and includes a long section that requires wading waist-deep in dark brown water stained with tannin from decayed vegetation. When we finally arrive I am exhausted, but the trackers are geared up for the forest and the gorilla trek. I gulp down a 2-litre bottle of water, wipe my brow and set off.

The effort is worth it. Once we have located the gorillas I concentrate on photographing the large silverback. He remains close by and for 40 minutes I shoot frame after frame. Then, with the long hike and the heat catching up with me, I sit down against a tree for a rest. A couple of minutes later, the silverback wanders over. He walks within a couple of metres of where I am sitting, lies down, puts his feet up on a tree and goes to sleep. When I leave, 20 minutes later, he is snoring.

ANIMALS ON THE EDGE: THE NEXT STEPS

As a photojournalist, most of my time is spent recording events. I draw plenty of conclusions from what I witness, but rarely do I have an opportunity to follow up with action to make a difference. The *Animals on the Edge* project has changed all that.

Many months ago I sat down in Los Angeles with a good friend, Leo Grillo. Like me, Leo is passionate about conservation and wildlife and, over a bottle of fine wine, we talked about the concept of the project and what it would take to turn theory into action.

That conversation led to the creation of *Animals on the Edge* as a not-for-profit programme of the NGO Living Earth. Its aim is to instigate community-based wildlife conservation schemes that minimize animal/human conflict and help impoverished people to benefit directly from the wildlife with which they coexist.

As this book goes to press, we are developing such programmes in India, Slovakia, Portugal and Borneo, thereby working to conserve species such as the Indian tiger, Tatra chamois, Iberian lynx and Bornean orangutan. In each case we are working with local people, helping them to realize a financial benefit from preserving wildlife and habitats, and thereby become less dependent on the profits of destructive exploitation of their natural resources.

For example, in Borneo we are working to develop an eco-tourism venture that will protect a large area of primary rainforest along the Kinabatangan River, providing employment for local villagers and enabling them to build a legacy that they can pass on to their children.

In India we are examining ways of developing a system of natural barriers that has proved successful in Africa. The intention is to bring these to farms and smallholdings that share their boundaries with major tiger preserves. This could help farmers increase productivity and reduce human/tiger conflict.

In Slovakia, we are working with Tatra National Park and the Tatra Foundation to help communities deal with predator encroachment. And in Portugal, in an effort to preserve the wildlife-rich habitats of the Alentejo, we are investigating ways of working with the European Union to develop a system similar to that operated by the Land Alliance in Brazil.

There is a lot of work to be done, but when I set about writing this book I had one overriding aim – I wanted my photography to make a difference. This project began in Los Angeles, home of Hollywood. And who knows, in Hollywood perhaps dreams really do come true.

Further information about *Animals on the Edge* can be found at the website www.animalsontheedge.org

ACKNOWLEDGMENTS

This book would have been impossible to produce without the input and help of a great many people. I hope I have remembered you all and, if not, then please accept that the omission of your name is simply down to an ageing memory rather than a lack of gratitude. I thank you all: IUCN and Species Survival Commission; Dr Jane Smart OBE; Nanda Rana; Latika Nath Rana; Singinawa Jungle Lodge; R.P. Singh; the Forest Department – Kanha National Park; Kohka Village Forest Committee; the team of mahouts in Kanha National Park; Chris Morgan; Cede Prudente; Carol Prudente; Jamal Bin Lias; Lias Bin Barapa; Sarala Aikanathan; Sepilok Orangutan Sanctuary; Dr Francine Neago; Labuk Bay Proboscis Monkey Sanctuary; Danum Valley Research Centre; Will Bolsover; Sabarata; Darma Budi; National Parks Authority – Gunung Leuser National Park; Bharatpur Police Department; Punya Bhandari; Temple Tiger Camp; the team of mahouts in Chitwan National Park; Assistant Warden – Chitwan National Park; Koshi Camp; the Warden – Koshi Tappu Wildlife Reserve; the Buffalo Soldiers – Anish Timsina, Rajilal Urav, Badai Chaudhari and Krisna Bidari; Julien Bayingana; Jean Marie Viommey Mfizi; Theoneste Mgerageze; the guides and trackers in Volcanoes National Park; Natalie Fynn; Taranjit Kaur; the guides and trackers in Mahale Mountains National Park; Andrew Conolly; Sarah Graham; Greg Bows; Marleen Lammers; Antelope Park; Pete Watmough; World Wildlife Fund – Congo and Central African Republic; Wildlife Conservation Society – Congo; the guides and trackers in Dzanga Ndoki National Park; the guides and trackers in Nouabale Ndoki National Park; Ngapé Anicet; Louis Sarna; the Ba'Aka pygmies; Gerald Manjuo; Apenheul Primate Park; Highland Wildlife Park; Slovak Tourist Board; Tatra National Park; Matthew Jevons; Terezia Rothova; Troy and Tracy Hyde; Astrid Vargas; Parque Nacional de Doñana; Dan Ward; Urs Breitenmoser; Jane Nicholson – Intro2020; Gray Levett – Grays of Westminster; Rick Fancett – Airdeal; Terry Hope; the team at Thames & Hudson; Art Wolfe; Christine Eckhoff; Deirdre Skillman; my long-suffering family, Claire and Josh; and my parents Mike and Beryl Weston.

And special thanks to my good friend, Leo Grillo – without you I'd never have made it beyond Heathrow.

CREDITS

All photos by Chris Weston, with the exception of:

Page 11 (top), 18, 19, 20–21, 24, 25, 26–27, 28–29, 30, 31, 34, 38, 39, 42–43, 66–67, 68–69, 70–71, 90, 91, 98–99, 102–3, 104, 105, 106–7, 108, 109, 110–11, 112, 114, 116, 117, 118, 119, 120–21, 122–23, 132, 134–35, 136–37, 138, 139, 140–41, 143, 166–67, 168–69, 174, 175, 176–77, 178, 179, 180–81, 182–83, 194–95, 196–97, 198–99, 200–1, 206: photos by Art Wolfe

Page 31: Satellite photo courtesy of NASA

Page 41: Photo © Alamy

Google Earth images reproduced courtesy of Google Earth Mapping Services:

Page 9: © 2007 Google™
© 2008 Europa Technologies,
Image © 2008 TerraMetrics
Page 13: © 2007 Google™
© 2008 Tele Atlas,
Image © 2008 DigitalGlobe
Page 220: © 2007 Google™
© 2008 Europa Technologies,
Image © 2008 TerraMetrics

Caption information in this book derives from the 2008 IUCN Red List of Threatened Species™. Contributors to the database are listed below:

Florida panther (puma, cougar)
Puma concolor coryi
Caso, A., Lopez-Gonzalez, C., Payan, E., Eizirik, E., de Oliveira, T., Leite-Pitman, R., Kelly, M., Valderrama, C., Lucherini, M.

Red wolf *Canis rufus*
Kelly, B.T., Beyer, A., Phillips, M.K.

Indiana bat *Myotis sodalis*
Arroyo-Cabrales, J., Ticul Alvarez Castaneda, S.

Black-headed spider monkey
Ateles fusciceps
Cuarón, A.D., Shedden, A., Rodríguez-Luna, E., de Grammont, P.C., Link, A.

Geoffroy's spider monkey
Ateles geoffroyi
Cuarón, A.D., Morales, A., Shedden, A., Rodriguez-Luna, E., de Grammont, P.C.

Yucatan black howler monkey
Alouatta pigra
Marsh, L.K., Cuarón, A.D., Cortés-Ortiz, L., Shedden, A., Rodríguez-Luna, E., de Grammont, P.C.

Golden lion tamarin
Leontopithecus rosalia
Kierulff, M.C.M., Rylands, A.B., de Oliveira, M.M.

Black lion tamarin
Leontopithecus chrysopygus
Kierulff, M.C.M., Rylands, A.B., Mendes. S.L., de Oliveira, M.M.

Golden-headed lion tamarin
Leontopithecus chrysomelas
Kierulff, M.C.M., Rylands, A.B., Mendes. S.L., de Oliveira, M.M.

Cotton-headed tamarin
Saguinus oedipus
Savage, A., Causado, J.

Giant otter *Pteronura brasiliensis*
Duplaix, N., Waldemarin, H.F., Groenedijk, J., Munis, M., Valesco, M., Botello, J.C.

Amur (Siberian) tiger
Panthera tigris ssp. *altaica*
Miquelle, D., Darman, Y., Seryodkin, I.

Iberian lynx *Lynx pardinus*
von Arx, M., Breitenmoser-Wursten, C.

Amur leopard *Panthera pardus orientalis*
Jackson, P., Nowell, K.

Tatra chamois *Rupicapra rupicapra tatrica*
Aulagnier, S., Giannatos, G., Herrero, J.

European bison (Lowland-Caucasian line)
Bison bonasus bonasus
Olech, W.

Sea otter *Enhydra lutris*
Doroff, A., Burdin, A.

Barbary macaque *Macaca sylvanus*
Butynski, T.M., Cortes, J., Waters, S., Fa, J., Hobbelink, M.E., van Lavieren, E., Belbachir, F., Cuzin, F., de Smet, K., Mouna, M., de Iongh, H., Menard, N., Camperio-Ciani, A.

Mountain gorilla
Gorilla beringei ssp. *beringei*
Robbins, M., Gray, M., Kümpel, N., Lanjouw, A., Maisels, F., Mugisha, A., Spelman, L., Williamson, L.

Western lowland gorilla
Gorilla gorilla ssp.*gorilla*
Walsh, P.D., Tutin, C.E.G., Baillie, J.E.M., Maisels, F., Stokes, E.J., Gatti, S.

Chimpanzee *Pan troglodytes*
Oates, J.F., Tutin, C.E.G., Humle, T., Wilson, M.L., Baillie, J.E.M., Balmforth, Z., Blom, A., Boesch, C., Cox, D., Davenport, T., Dunn, A., Dupain, J., Duvall, C., Ellis, C.M., Farmer, K.H., Gatti, S., Greengrass, E., Hart, J., Herbinger, I., Hicks, C., Hunt, K.D., Kamenya, S., Maisels, F., Mitani, J.C., Moore, J., Morgan, B.J., Morgan, D.B., Nakamura, M., Nixon, S., Plumptre, A.J., Reynolds, V., Stokes, E.J., Walsh, P.D.

Bonobo *Pan paniscus*
Fruth, B., Benishay, J.M., Bila-Isia, I., Coxe, S., Dupain, J., Furuichi, T., Hart, J., Hart, T., Hashimoto, C., Hohmann, G., Hurley, M., Ilambu, O., Mulavwa, M., Ndunda, M., Omasombo, V., Reinartz, G., Scherlis, J., Steel, L., Thompson, J.

Painted hunting dog *Lycaon pictus*
McNutt, J.W., Mills, M.G.L., McCreery, K., Rasmussen, G., Robbins, R., Woodroffe, R.

Black rhinoceros *Diceros bicornis*
IUCN SSC African Rhino Specialist Group

Grevy's zebra *Equus grevyi*
Moehlman, P.D., Rubenstein, D.I., Kebede, F.

Drill *Mandrillus leucophaeus*
Oates, J.F., Butynski, T.M.

Golden-crowned sifaka
Propithecus tattersalli
Andrainarivo, C., Andriaholinirina, V.N., Feistner, A., Felix, T., Ganzhorn, J., Garbutt, N., Golden, C., Konstant, B., Louis Jr., E., Meyers, D., Mittermeier, R.A., Perieras, A., Princee, F., Rabarivola, J.C., Rakotosamimanana B., Rasamimanana, H., Ratsimbazafy, J., Raveloarinoro, G., Razafimanantsoa, A., Rumpler, Y., Schwitzer, C., Thalmann, U., Wilmé, L., Wright, P.

Crowned sifaka
Propithecus coronatus
Andrainarivo, C., Andriaholinirina, V.N., Feistner, A., Felix, T., Ganzhorn, J., Garbutt, N., Golden, C., Konstant, B., Louis Jr., E., Meyers, D., Mittermeier, R.A., Perieras, A., Princee, F., Rabarivola, J.C., Rakotosamimanana, B., Rasamimanana, H., Ratsimbazafy, J., Raveloarinoro, G., Razafimanantsoa, A., Rumpler, Y., Schwitzer, C., Thalmann, U., Wilmé, L., Wright, P.

Black-and-white ruffed lemur
Varecia variegata
Andrainarivo, C., Andriaholinirina, V.N., Feistner, A., Felix, T., Ganzhorn, J., Garbutt, N., Golden, C., Konstant, B., Louis Jr., E., Meyers, D., Mittermeier, R.A., Perieras, A., Princee, F., Rabarivola, J.C., Rakotosamimanana, B., Rasamimanana, H., Ratsimbazafy, J., Raveloarinoro, G., Razafimanantsoa, A., Rumpler, Y., Schwitzer, C., Thalmann, U., Wilmé, L., Wright, P.

Red ruffed lemur *Varecia rubra*
Andrainarivo, C., Andriaholinirina, V.N., Feistner, A., Felix, T., Ganzhorn, J., Garbutt, N., Golden, C., Konstant, B., Louis Jr., E., Meyers, D., Mittermeier, R.A., Perieras, A., Princee, F., Rabarivola, J.C., Rakotosamimanana, B., Rasamimanana, H., Ratsimbazafy, J., Raveloarinoro, G., Razafimanantsoa, A., Rumpler, Y., Schwitzer, C., Thalmann, U., Wilmé, L., Wright, P.

Diademed sifaka
Propithecus diadema
Andrainarivo, C., Andriaholinirina, V.N., Feistner, A., Felix, T., Ganzhorn, J., Garbutt, N., Golden, C., Konstant, B., Louis Jr., E., Meyers, D., Mittermeier, R.A., Perieras, A., Princee, F., Rabarivola, J.C., Rakotosamimanana, B., Rasamimanana, H., Ratsimbazafy, J., Raveloarinoro, G., Razafimanantsoa, A., Rumpler, Y., Schwitzer, C., Thalmann, U., Wilmé, L., Wright, P.

Indri *Indri indri*
Andrainarivo, C., Andriaholinirina, V.N., Feistner, A., Felix, T., Ganzhorn, J., Garbutt, N., Golden, C., Konstant, B., Louis Jr., E., Meyers, D., Mittermeier, R.A., Perieras, A., Princee, F., Rabarivola, J.C., Rakotosamimanana, B., Rasamimanana, H., Ratsimbazafy, J., Raveloarinoro, G., Razafimanantsoa, A., Rumpler, Y., Schwitzer, C., Thalmann, U., Wilmé, L., Wright, P.

Aye-aye *Daubentonia madagascariensis*
Andrainarivo, C., Andriaholinirina, V.N., Feistner, A., Felix, T., Ganzhorn, J., Garbutt, N., Golden, C., Konstant, B., Louis Jr., E., Meyers, D., Mittermeier, R.A., Perieras, A., Princee, F., Rabarivola, J.C., Rakotosamimanana, B., Rasamimanana, H., Ratsimbazafy, J., Raveloarinoro, G., Razafimanantsoa, A., Rumpler, Y., Schwitzer, C., Thalmann, U., Wilmé, L., Wright, P.

Pygmy hippopotamus
Choeropsis liberiensis
Lewison, R., Oliver, W.

Snow leopard *Panthera uncia*
Jackson, R., Mallon, D., McCarthy, T., Chundaway, R.A., Habib, B.

Markhor *Capra falconeri*
Valdez, R.

Wild Bactrian camel *Camelus ferus*
Hare, J.

Giant panda *Ailuropoda melanoleuca*
Lü, Z., Wang, D., Garshelis, D.L.

Red panda *Ailurus fulgens*
Wang, X., Choudhry, A., Yonzon, P., Wozencraft, C., Than Zaw

Upland barasingha
Rucervus duvaucelii branderi
Duckworth, J.W., Samba Kumar, N., Chiranjibi Prasad Pokheral, Sagar Baral, H., Timmins, R.J.

Red slender loris *Loris tardigradus*
Nekaris, A.

Lion-tailed macaque
Macaca silenus
Kumar, A., Singh, M., Molur, S.

Greater one-horned rhinoceros
Rhinoceros unicornis
Talukdar, B.K., Emslie, R., Bist, S.S., Choudhury, A., Ellis, S., Bonal, B.S., Malakar, M.C., Talukdar, B.N., Barua, M.

Asian elephant *Elephas maximus*
Choudhury, A., Lahiri Choudhury, D.K., Desai, A., Duckworth, J.W., Easa, P.S., Johnsingh, A.J.T., Fernando, P., Hedges, S., Gunawardena, M., Kurt, F., Karanth, U., Lister, A., Menon, V., Riddle, H., Rübel, A., Wikramanayake, E.

Tiger *Panthera tigris*
Chundawat, R.S., Habib, B., Karanth, U., Kawanishi, K., Ahmad Khan, J., Lynam, T., Miquelle, D., Nyhus, P., Sunarto, Tilson, R., Sonam Wang

Wild Asiatic water buffalo
Bubalus arnee
Hedges, S., Sagar Baral, H., Timmins, R.J., Duckworth, J.W.

Northern white-cheeked gibbon
Nomascus leucogenys
Bleisch, B., Geissmann,T., Manh Ha, N., Rawson, B., Timmins, R.J.

Lar gibbon *Hylobates lar*
Brockelman, W., Geissmann, T.

Silvery Javan gibbon
Hylobates moloch
Andayani, N., Brockelman, W., Geissmann, T., Nijman, V., Supriatna, J.

Celebes crested macaque
Macaca nigra
Supriatna, J., Andayani, N.

Red-shanked douc langur
Pygathrix nemaeus
Ngoc Thanh, V., Lippold, L., Timmins, R.J., Manh Ha, N.

Bornean orangutan
Pongo pygmaeus
Ancrenaz, M., Marshall, A., Goossens, B., van Schaik, C., Sugardjito, J., Gumal, M., Wich, S.

Proboscis monkey *Nasalis larvatus*
Meijaard, E., Nijman, V., Supriatna, J.

Borneo bay cat *Pardofelis badia*
Hearn, A., Sanderson, J., Ross, J., Wilting, A., Sunarto, S.

Sumatran rhinoceros
Dicerorhinus sumatrensis
van Strien, N.J., Manullang, B., Sectionov, Isnan, W., Khan, M.K.M, Sumardja, E., Ellis, S., Han, K.H., Boeadi, Payne, J., Bradley Martin, E.

Javan rhinoceros
Rhinoceros sondaicus
van Strien, N.J., Steinmetz, R., Manullang, B., Sectionov, Han, K.H., Isnan, W., Rookmaaker, K., Sumardja, E., Khan, M.K.M., Ellis, S.

Sumatran orangutan *Pongo abelii*
Singleton, I., Wich, S.A., Griffiths, M.

Other sources cited in the text

Page 15: *National Geographic*, November 2008, 'Borneo's Moment of Truth'.
Pages 30–31: *Panorama: Can Money Grow on Trees?* BBC documentary broadcast in UK on 8 September 2008.
Page 152: *Satya*, May 2005.
Page 164: Employment statistics from *Conservation of the Tiger*, doctoral thesis by Dr Latika Nath Rana.